T0156628

WHAT *IS*
HAPPENING?

WHAT *IS* HAPPENING?

GERRY AGNEW

TRUE DIRECTIONS
AN AFFILIATE OF TARCHER BOOKS

iUniverse

WHAT IS HAPPENING?

iUniverse books may be ordered through booksellers or by contacting:

iUniverse
1663 Liberty Drive
Bloomington, IN 47403
www.iuniverse.com
1-800-Authors (1-800-288-4677)

Because of the dynamic nature of the Internet, any web addresses or links contained in this book may have changed since publication and may no longer be valid. The views expressed in this work are solely those of the author and do not necessarily reflect the views of the publisher, and the publisher hereby disclaims any responsibility for them.

Any people depicted in stock imagery provided by Thinkstock are models, and such images are being used for illustrative purposes only. Certain stock imagery © Thinkstock.

ISBN: 978-1-4917-5714-7 (sc)
ISBN: 978-1-4917-5713-0 (e)

Library of Congress Control Number: 2014922710

Printed in the United States of America.

iUniverse rev. date: 01/19/2015

Acknowledgments

Behind every author (hopefully a successful one here!) lies his friends and family—people who care and have egged him on with his venture. I have been blessed with three such people, and I wish you to be aware whom you can credit (or curse) for the effort that follows. Why is it that when you need people like this around you, they appear as if by magic?

I wish to thank, with all my heart, my long-suffering wife, who finally got me off my intellectual duff and told me, "Write the book, dammit." I have been married to her for nearly forty years now, and she *still* has to talk like this to get me going. There is no question that without her, this book would not have been written.

My thanks to my granddaughter, Shylee, who continually encouraged me to put the ideas I had been talking to her about into some sort of format that made sense. She got me organized and put the ideas into a meaningful pattern from the chaos they were in before. Wise beyond her twenty years, she told me, "You have good information. Get it out to as many people as possible." Thank you, Shylee!

Finally, to a wise woman named Lisa Boag-Guidi, who is a veritable font of ideas, I give my sincere thanks. When I was talking to her about the book and wondering how I should get the relevant ideas together, she merely asked, "Why don't you divide the book into several segments and then expand each one?" Such a simple idea and one that I am sure would never have occurred to me if I was left to my own devices. The best ideas are the simplest. Thank you, Lisa!

Introduction
Why Are You So Ensnared in
Today's Financial World?

I have been considering writing a book ever since my granddaughter suggested it. At that time I was busy in my retirement, writing a newsletter devoted to global financial and cultural matters. My granddaughter can be very persuasive, however.

In my many years in the financial markets, culminating as a senior foreign-exchange advisor with Bank of America in Seattle, Washington (I am a Canadian citizen), I came to the conclusion that what we are seeing and hearing about our globalized economy could be assessed via a thorough study of economics and what makes it work. This is a study of how a particular culture influences what we see and consider about such trends. My granddaughter, and then the rest of my family, suggested that I could reach many more people than I could with a simple newsletter.

I agreed with this, and so was born *What* Is *Happening?* In my book I wish to tell people, based on my forty-plus years of financial experience, why they are feeling so caught by what they read every day in their favorite medium. It seems that whatever our leaders, politicians, and financial specialists tell us, nothing ever seems to get better.

We suffer from squeezed incomes, and whatever we try to do to enjoy what our societies offer us, we can never fully savor the fruits of our labors. Debt mounts up as we borrow to bridge the differences between our wants and our incomes. And throughout all of this, we constantly read about the CEO of a major corporation enjoying yet another multimillion-dollar bonus. This lucky person enjoys such riches for apparently doing little more than firing thousands of local workers and sending the jobs to China, Cambodia, Bangladesh, or someplace that many of us have never heard of.

New records are set with the number of freshly minted billionaires increasing every year, while we slog along wondering how the dentist bills are going to be paid.

Resting up after a crippling leg injury suffered last September in the aftermath of the High River floods, I chanced to reacquaint myself with the analysis of a noted financial author who has been in the business for decades: Marty Armstrong. The man is a genius in my view, and he has discovered that markets operate according to various cycles.

No, nothing new there, but he showed again and again that a multiple of pi (i.e., the 3.1416 number we learned about in high school to discover the area of a circle given its radius) dominates many of the financial markets we see. His hypothesis was a simple one. We should forget the hyperbole surrounding what the financial press says about financial panics, as the various reporting media tend to be swept up in the emotions of the moment. All of what we see can be defined on longer-term considerations, he says, and that is what we should be looking at.

Fascinated, and bedridden with little to occupy my time, I started to wonder if our culture itself could be subject to the same pi cycle. Remarkably, I think that it *can*. I started with a very old template (the Bible) for the principles that America was supposed to be founded on: a Christian nation that is subject to cycles. This we have apparently been warned about for thousands of years.

No, please do not roll your eyeballs at this mention of the Bible (which is what another of my daughters did when I told her about this project). Hear me out. You have not wasted your money in buying this book—really and truly!

Without some sort of mathematical proof of what I am writing about, I might agree with you and indulge in eyeball-rolling myself. But there *is* proof, and thanks to the idea I obtained from Mr. Armstrong, I decided to go ahead with all that I am about to show you. I would like to give you one small example of what lies ahead in chapter 1.

I simply cannot believe that all of what follows is a mathematical coincidence. Look up the Old Testament, in particular Daniel 8:14, where the two angels are talking about 2,300 "mornings and evenings." I started to play with pi on my handheld calculator and found the following—with pi valued here at 3.14159 (my calculator won't go any higher than five decimal places).

2,300/3.14159/3.14159 = 233.039. Now, 233 is a Fibonacci number, which means it is part of a sequence formed by adding the two previous whole numbers together, starting at 1 (i.e., 1, 2, 3, 5, 8, 13, 21, 34, 89, 144, 233, etc.). I also found out that the number 233 ties in beautifully with the story of the United States and its founding in 1776. Want to see more? Go to the Bible and pi section of segment 1, and read what it says about the next few years.

Fibonacci analyses, by the way, are very useful for equity (stock market) traders in assessing various heights and depths of markets and, after a rise (or fall), just how far a rebound can come. In other words, they are not an idle curiosity but something with real usefulness for a major trader.

They also have a very good practical benefit in assessing the future of the United States (and the Western world, as it is all tied together via the large-scale use of the American dollar, the world's reserve currency). Anyhow, have a look at what I have found, as it does tie in with the thesis of this book.

Let us continue with the 2,300 analysis. We take 2,300/233.039 and arrive at 9.86596. Divide this by 3.14159, and we get (drumroll) … 3.14159, pi almost exactly! This caught my attention, and with plenty of time to analyze other possible biblical pi cycles, I certainly had the opportunity to do so. There is a *great* deal more, interestingly enough, and I shall be putting this in chapter 1 for your perusal.

There are many other ideas I wish to share with you, and you can read them in the remaining chapters of this book. There are sections on oil and politics, which also include a good look at the giant tar sands in Alberta, Canada (my home province), and how it can affect what you pay for your weekly (or more frequent) fill-up at the pump.

It also says a lot about how the Western world operates, given that so much revolves around the price of this critical commodity. What about US politics, and what can we say about the possibility of a President Hillary Clinton?

Ah, there is so much to help you understand *What Is Happening?*

SEGMENT 1

CHAPTER 1

The Genius of Marty Armstrong and Some Biblical Pi (No, Not Pie!)

I have mentioned the redoubtable Marty Armstrong already in the introduction to this book, but it occurs to me that many of you have no idea who the man is. I had better explain, hadn't I?

He is an analyst *par excellence* and was responsible (although he probably doesn't know it in the least) for my finding the extraordinary examples of how pi and Fibonacci analysis are seen in the books of Daniel and Revelation in the Bible. He also has found the economic properties of the number 4.3 (more commonly expressed as twice this, as a cycle based of 8.6 times a unit of time—generally a year).

He found this, apparently, by looking at the time which it takes for the Earth, as measured by the long-term movement of the North Pole, to make a full circle in the sky at night. This takes 25,800 years and is an exact multiple of 8.6— 3,000 times. Now, I have no idea why such a huge number of years has an effect on much smaller cycles, such as what he analyzes for his readers, but it does. As such, I would be foolish not to take note of what he says and has proved.

I do not use this number to assess my biblical pi cycles, but it is with great interest I see that what I come up with and what he derives are close to exact in assessing the future. My biblical cycles and his pi and 8.6 ("polar cycle," to give it a name) show that we must pay close attention to his discovery and how he has determined it has such an effect in the real world.

I have never seen him refer to the Bible for his work, but of interest is a moment in Daniel 12:11 that says, "From the time that the daily sacrifice is abolished and the abomination that causes desolation is set up, there will be 1,290 days." The next verse speaks of those people being happy who will persevere until the 1,335th day. This tells us that what Armstrong has found has biblical significance, because 1,290 is exactly divisible by 8.6—150 times.

No, I do not know (yet) what the 150 stands for. But I also note that 1,335 is almost an exact pi multiple. So why did the angel advising Daniel tell him about 1,290 days? Why did he inform him about 1,335 days? Why did the angel use these apparently strange numbers (as opposed to something like 1,300 and 1,350—something "nice and round")?

There is clearly something significant relating to these "strange numbers," and the answer must clearly be that they are both to be seen in a cycle and that, possibly without knowing about it, Armstrong has stumbled into a set of cycles which are, in effect, ratified by the Bible. Is this why they are so accurate and why he is so highly sought after to advise nations like China?

I shall also make references, as the reader will see as he or she progresses throughout the various segments and chapters, to Armstrong's major work: the war cycle. This horrible thing he has worked on for a long time, and apparently it goes back, in one form or another, for centuries.

It shows, for a reason which I do not fully understand, that mankind engages in war—either directly or indirectly— every quarter century. I do not mean a life-and-death struggle for the very fate of the human race, but rather we see one of three things: a major conflict, a medium-sized one (à la Korea), or else a major change of a dominant philosophy somewhere in the world that has a major global impact.

Let me give you an example of this, just dating back to the early twentieth century. In 1914, and we see the centenary of this in 2014, was the First World War (the Great War, as it is known in Britain), which started in August of that year (*The Guns of August* is a major work describing this terrible conflict). In 1939, just after the end of August, we saw the German invasion of Poland, which started the Second World War. That is to say, twenty-five years after 1914.

In August 1964, we saw a major decision by the powers that be in the United States (then at the very zenith of its global authority politically, culturally, and economically) to start the ball in motion for the desperately expensive and divisive war in Southeast Asia: Vietnam.

At that time, the Pentagon carried out what we might describe today as a False Flag operation in the Gulf of Tonkin, which led to the first US incursions into that country early in 1965 (after the presidential election in November 1964, the cynic might add). In 1989 there was no war, but the collapse of communism under the last significant Soviet leader Mikhail Gorbachev would certainly qualify as a major change in how the world is run, in my book.

As an aside here, I should note that many people (me among them, as I have written about in my newsletter) feel that the collapse of communism was some sort of "staged event" and that some years down the road we shall see it, or a close cousin, reemerge.

Now we come to 2014, which is, as noted, the centenary of World War I. It is a war cycle year, and while we came close to something happening in Syria and the Middle East in 2013, the cycles were not correct then. We have moved to 2014, where the ongoing ruckus in the Ukraine (as this is being written) is threatening to explode into all sorts of nasty things.

We should look for something to happen in the last six months of this year, as Armstrong has pointed out that this time of the year is not friendly to peace. Yep, have to agree with this one. Japan is also, for the first time since its shattering defeat in World War II, starting to flex its muscles in its area of the Pacific, and one wonders if there will be a clash between Japan and China before all of this is over. There might also be a clash in Korea again.

What defined Korea was its liberation from Japanese colonial oppression in 1945. The years 2014–1945 = 69 years, which almost exactly twenty-two times pi. Twenty-two is a number that I find very interesting as well, as we shall see just a little later on. I am left wondering if a sixty-nine-year gap in conflicts is also something we should carefully access as we move forward. Just for fun, 69/22 is also almost equal to pi (22 × 3.1416 = 69.115). Powerful stuff here! *Please note that as the book goes on, I refer to "pi numbers." A pi number is one that is almost exactly divisible by pi, and this means a great deal in my system of biblical pi analysis!*

I shall refer to Armstrong's work as I look at various economic cycles as they play out in the United States. Remember that because of the primacy of the US dollar across the world, it remains the world's reserve currency—a place where governments store their reserve cash. What transpires in New York City and Washington is of critical importance as we move toward whatever awaits us.

In particular, I am looking at Armstrong's date of October 1, 2015, where he writes that his study of cycles tells him that we are looking at an event that will cause the world's sovereign bond markets (where global governments go to borrow the funds they need for day-to-day operations) to start to implode. Now, how many times have we read about how the United States is in serious straits because it borrows so much? What do you think will happen if it becomes difficult for the US Treasury to raise the funds it requires?

It will not be good, and Armstrong feels that while this unfortunate cycle starts to becomes deeper and more painful, it will probably spill over to the rest of the world. By the way, in looking at Armstrong's October 1, 2015, date, I looked at my biblical pi cycles and found that all of this nastiness starts on October 14, 2015. This is clearly very close to Armstrong's date (and I shall detail all of what I have found in this segment of the book), and we must pay close attention in how he and I look at all of this.

Armstrong has been in this business for a long time, and in the 1980s he was so good at what he did that he could demand, and receive, sums to make him the highest paid economist in the United States (Wikipedia).

He was arrested and jailed for seven years for contempt, and the rumor mill is that he would not give to US authorities his techniques for his exceptionally accurate forecasting analysis. Rightly or wrongly, he is now out of custody and is forecasting yet again. It is these most recent calls which we shall be interested in for the first segment of this book.

He is, perhaps understandably, bitter toward the economic and political future of the United States. I leave what he has to say to my readers to assess for themselves. All I can do is to deeply analyze what I believe lies ahead using my own analysis, which is what this book is all about.

❖ ❖ ❖

All right, I have written fairly extensively on Mr. Armstrong. However, this is my book, and you may be asking—justifiably—where do I get all of the information I am going to present to you in the coming chapters?

In the main, I have simply referred to the newsletters that I send out to my readers five times a week. For these, when I was writing them, I did a fair piece of research, and so I believe that they are accurate as to the date they were written. In any event, the purpose of this book is the same as when I wrote my newsletters: to try to make a reader think and consider what might lie ahead and therefore see that there may be other possibilities to consider going forward.

There are two sides to every story, and while it is so nice and easy to simply pick up the daily newspaper (online or otherwise) and browse the editorial to see what the "correct" thinking is, I would like readers to consider other possibilities. They may amaze you!

In any event, I have written several segments to make up this book. They will comprise the look at the biblical analysis I have been referring to. Within this first segment, there will be various chapters looking at the math of pi and Fibonacci analysis. Why is this? I firmly believe that a book on this subject must present more than just "Daniel means this or that" or "Revelation really means something very different because … just because."

If I fail to deliver on the mathematical analysis to the reader's satisfaction, so be it. I am still going to try, and other chapters in this first segment will carry on this belief of mine. Other segments will be divided into chapters as well, and they will deal with oil (*the* biggie as we move forward) and the attempts to procure ever more of this critical commodity by the powers that be in Washington. And that is probably quite enough for segment 1, chapter 1!

CHAPTER 2

Let's Have Some Fibonacci Pi!

No, no—not that kind of pie! I am not talking about some unusual fruit confection but rather the mathematical variety. This is the number 3.1416 (although it is a mathematical expression that goes on forever) which, if we multiply it by the diameter of a circle, we find a very close approximation of its circumference. Isn't the idea of a circle somehow appropriate, given that we are looking at financial and cultural cycles?

If indeed this *is* appropriate, then why shouldn't (as I have been hinting at so far) we use pi to further tell our tale of a series of terrible occurrences soon to hit the United States and the world through the mechanism of the US dollar being the global reserve currency? We can, and now we shall.

To establish the validity of pi (which I stumbled across while convalescing last October), I looked at the 2,300 "mornings and evenings" in Daniel. Recently, I looked at this again and found another pi link. Let's revisit the number

2,300 and wonder how many years it actually is. The key thing here is how people back then measured a year.

The best I could come up with was 366 days, which was used in Rome when various climatologists (and I use the term very loosely when measured against what people today can do with similar sets of data) had to work out the length of a year.

This 366 number will not work over long periods of time, as distortions will build and impact planting seasons and so forth. Nevertheless, I used it, as it is probably the frame of reference that mankind had when the angels made their divine call for the 2,300 mornings and evenings. It turns out that 2,300/366 = 6.2842. Twice pi equals 6.2832, which is extremely close indeed. A difference of just 0.016 percent is hardly worth mentioning!

It made me wonder again about whether two times pi can be found in other bits and pieces of end-times analysis, and (you guessed it) it *can*. Even more interesting is that it directly relates to timelines found in Armstrong's financial crisis date. It is my contention that the end-times, lying directly ahead, relate to a major financial disturbance (there is definitely a "disturbance in the Force" here).

We are not looking at a coincidence. The writers of the Bible have placed before us, if we can find these things (and I am sure that I have barely scratched the surface with my rather fortunate discoveries to date), a very interesting commentary on our future that was written millennia ago. There is one other bit of seeming trivia here in Daniel. One of the angels addressing Daniel said that the contents of what Daniel was told were to remained "sealed up until the time of the end." If my book is helping to unseal them, and I give sincere thanks to Higher Beings, then surely it is yet another indication that our immediate future is what Daniel was shown.

Now let me make a few references to my newsletter on this subject. Immediately, I wish to start assessing what this financial crisis could be and what are the relevant dates that accompany such a disaster. Let us simply say that for now it is fairly easy to see that the cause for our troubles must be the monster called debt.

I know that the average American has borrowed himself or herself into oblivion over the past few decades, and all of this was probably done to maintain a standard of living that people apparently felt they were, in some sense, owed. I cannot debate the validity of such a belief; I can merely note it with regret. This grave concern must stem from the huge debts being run up with monster interest rates that can only act as a severe drag on the economy.

That is, of course, only one element of the US debt burden. We must also consider the accumulated debts of municipal and state spending (which is considerable), and then we come to Washington's contribution to all of this insanity. Is this the right word?

Unfortunately, it is. With Congress showing all of the backbone of a wet noodle, we are ballooning the debt level to $17.5 trillion as of April 24, 2014. It is this we hear about all the time with the GOP in Congress declaiming the Democratic White House. Unfortunately, the reverse is also true, as administrations from both parties seem to outdo themselves in wild and irresponsible spending. It is not getting any better, sorry to say, and will probably get worse, especially if the economy continues to waffle endlessly in the aftermath of the 2007–8 mortgage debacle.

I rant and rave about all of this, but it seems that if this monster debt burden comes adrift, it would be the cause of the disaster that I think Daniel and Revelation are both looking at. The latter book suggests that debt and its corrupting influence will be a killer for the economy and society in general. We shall examine this a bit later on.

It is what Armstrong has been looking at, as have I. I am scared to death, to be honest, but if all of this was seen with an angel talking to St. John on the Island of Patmos in about the year AD 95, then the momentum building toward a dissolution of this debt (and its knock-on equivalents across the globe, do not forget) must be incredible and completely unstoppable.

Let's finish off this chapter with some more pi and Fibonacci analysis for you. Oh dear! I wish all of the sorrow which I am writing about *were* a nice piece of Fibonacci pie! I have no idea what that would taste like, but surely it has to be better than the bitter taste now in my mouth!

I think the best way to proceed would be explaining what 233 is and how it relates to the United States specifically. Well, it is a major Fibonacci number used in financial (equity/stock market) analysis, as we saw earlier. It directly relates to the United States, and we saw this in my cursory analysis about Daniel in the introduction. Now let us look at the founding of the United States, which traditionally dates from the signing and publicizing of the Declaration of Independence on July 4, 1776.

If we take this date and move forward 233 years, we come to 2009. Return to the comments of the "twice pi" argument above, which related to the 2,300 mornings and evenings. This prophecy equates to twice pi when converted to years on a 366-day basis. In terms of years (again) this is six years, 102 days. Adding this onto July 4, 2009, we come to October 14–15, 2015, which is just about what Armstrong's date of October 1, 2015 is! This is quite beyond the realm of coincidence, in my mind. Let us explore this a bit further to finish off this chapter.

Fibonacci analysis is very good for analytical work in stocks and equities, as we have discussed. However, how accurate is this in reality for the average person to read these lines and nod in agreement? The rule of thumb is that we have a precise Fibonacci target year, in this case 1776 + 233, or 2009, but rounding and the like can occur and mess things up, but only a little bit.

Therefore, I can say that for the purposes of this work *all* analysis must fall within a plus-or-minus-one-year band. For this Fibonacci analysis to be valid, it cannot occur before 2008 or after 2010, which is still a fairly narrow band. In 2008, we see the real start to the mortgage debacle (the so-called subprime lending crisis), which made financial headlines across the world.

In 2010 we saw the bottom of a secondary bear market that this banker foolishness started (the primary bottom was, of course, in the Fibonacci year 2009). So we have good dates to look at the current financial difficulties in the world (for we are still seeing bad balance sheets from the 2008 collapse; the proof of this is the huge amount of fed money being poured into the financial system month after month). Therefore, 2009 is not out of the question as an accurate US end date for the 233 Fibonacci number analysis.

The October 14–15, 2015, date is also reasonable. This is, of course, unless Armstrong and I are both out to lunch on all of this and the theory of pi cycles is wrong. To be honest, I do not agree to my missing of lunch in the least. Pi is correct!

Let's push on to more (and meatier) pi and Fibonacci analysis in chapter 3 of this first segment. I wish to write about political instability in the United States and some dates you may wish to mark down. I am not happy with what lies ahead, and we shall now see what sorts of pi analysis can be used to tell you what is probably going to be what.

CHAPTER 3

Let's Have Some More Fibonacci Pi! (Appetite Still There?)

If you thought that all of what I had to offer you on biblical analysis (particularly as it has to do with market crashes and the like) was written in chapter 2, you might also think that what moves the stock markets overall and (by extension) the US economy, is something which is completely random. By definition, therefore, it cannot be known by either traders or regular citizens. You would be wrong!

There is an old saying that "there is a divinity that shapes our ends," and I can think of nothing better to demonstrate this than by a long-term analysis of what the stock market has done since 1953. Yes, as you may have guessed by now, this date is directly derived from America's founding date of 1776 and directly related to a simple derivative of (what else?) pi.

Let me now quote from my newsletter—two of them, actually—in which I looked at all of this in some depth. It is amazing what is to be found from the simple number 3.1416. I wonder how much else lies out there for the enterprising reader to find? (Go for it!)

Note that the mathematical symbols used seem to be fairly standard. However, let me simply say that $\pi^{0.5}$ is the square root of pi, $\pi^{0.3333}$ is the cube root, and $\pi^{0.25}$ is the fourth root. A square root is a number which when multiplied by itself comes to pi, a cube root is a number which when multiplied by itself three times come to pi, and so on. Let's see what I wrote:

> Late last year I wrote for the newsletter a series of articles on the number pi (i.e., 3.1416) and how it related to the book of Daniel in the Old Testament and to the book of Revelation in the New. I looked at various interesting possibilities (all based off a chance bit of analysis I performed on Daniel's 2,300 "mornings and evenings," which is to be found in Daniel 8:14).

> There were some curious yet fundamental Fibonacci numbers (233 in the main), which seem to be intimately tied together with the current history of the United States. When added to dates from America's early founding—principally 1776—these numbers gave some very notable results.

> These essays from last year can now be referred to as "ancient history," but again, quite by chance, I found some more unexpected things that tell of US history in the early twentieth

century and early twenty-first. Perhaps there is indeed a Divinity that shapes our ends!

When I wrote about these pi cycles initially, I thought there was something else but didn't know what it was. Now I do (I think so, anyway). I was watching the first of the movie series *Twilight* a few weeks ago when the hero of the movie talked briefly about 1.7725, which the leading lady then identified as the square root of pi. Idly, I then started to play with my calculator and looked at the square, cube, and fourth roots of pi. The following is what I found.

$\pi = 3.1416$

$\pi^{0.5} = 1.7725$

$\pi^{0.3333} = 1.466$ (reasonable, as my calculator does not have cube root buttons)

$\pi^{0.25} = 1.331$

I also saw (and this provided me with the idea to move along in this vein) that some Fibonacci numbers are directly related to pi in multiples.

For example, 987 is a Fibonacci number, and $100(\pi^2)$ almost exactly equals this! (Get out your calculator and have a look.) Additionally, in using Fibonacci analysis, we can use this sort of thing for cycles. For example, we can use the first significant digits in such analysis, so the above pi functions can be used as 177, 146, and 133.

This is what we often see in such analysis. Coincidentally, we see that the number above in the 987 analysis and π^2 (i.e., 100) is used to move the decimal two places to the right in the pi roots above (i.e., 177, 146, and 133). It makes them nearly equal in current history, other words. Is this important? Very definitely it is! Please keep reading tomorrow.

Then, the next day, I wrote as follows:

In my original pi cycle analysis, I looked at the year 1776 and added 233 and so forth. This is all correct, but now we see that there are other possibilities.

1,776 + 133 = 1,909. It is clear that the roots of pi (i.e., square, cube, and fourth roots as above) and the date 1776 are all interlinked. Therefore, the founding of the United States is of critical importance to the world going forward and has always been so as it gathered its strength in moving toward the seminal period now upon us. Let's look at some numbers now.

1909 + standard Fibonacci numbers, in a series:

1909 + 5 = 1914. World War I, which really started to change the face of the earth.

1909 + 8 = 1917. The United States commits itself to this great change in the world by joining the Great War. The Russian Revolution occurs and communism takes over that country.

1909 + 13 = 1922. I am not sure what this date represents, even after all sorts of research. *But*, 1776 + 146 (cube root of pi) = 1922. We can then say, once again, that pi numbers are inextricably linked to the immediate future history (if this is not a paradox) of the United States. I can go one step further.

The United States is *so* important to the world (principally through the mechanism of the dollar as the world's reserve currency) that what happens to this nation is going to have major impacts on the rest of the planet. I think this is the message of the Revelation as shown to St. John on Patmos.

How can I continue to apparently obsess over this financial angle? Well, have a look at the amazing Fibonacci numbers a couple of paragraphs below (scaled off the year 1953)—*all* of which are related by the founding of the United States in 1776.

To finish the current table, we see

1909 + 21 = 1930. Great Depression and major secondary stock market crash—*the* Crash, in many respects.

1909 + 34 = 1943. Year (plus one) of first controlled nuclear reaction in Chicago (and consequent development of the atomic bomb).

1909 + 55 = 1964. Height of US empire financially, economically, and militarily, and the Gulf of Tonkin crisis (also a war cycle year), which started the United States on its current monetary difficulties.

Oh, yes! Let's play with your mind a little bit here. We are currently observing the centenary of the start of World War I. It is clear to my numbers-obsessed mind that the year 2014/15 could well be monumental. Now let us assess the financial problems related to 1776 and another root value of pi (the fourth root, in this case) to finish off this essay tomorrow.

The next day I finished off this new pi cycle material as follows:

Consider 177–133 (one level of pi subtracted from another) and we get 44. Now, 1,909 + 44 = 1,953, and I have been told by someone who has studied this for many years (now sadly deceased) that the major prophecies in the Great Pyramid came to an end in ... the year 1953! I also note that this is related to the founding of the United States and is the sum of 1776 + 177.

More than coincidence? This person also told me that the prophecies in the Great Pyramid mentioned the crash of the stock market in 1929–30. What he *didn't* tell me was that the rest of the major market crashes in US market history are *all* related to this number. The following table now tells me that what lies ahead for the United States and the world are financial in nature. The numbers and dates are all tops or crashes, which does not look good going forward at all.

Have a look (as noted from above):

1953 + 5 = 1958, or a major recession year in the United States.

1953 + 8 = 1961. Now, nothing happened this year, but 1962 (Fibonacci + one is allowable) was a very bad year.

1953 + 13 = 1966, or the top of the US stock market for decades to come in real terms. A major top, in other words.

1953 + 21 = 1974. Major market decline in an overbought market amid the oil-related effects from the Gulf War.

1953 + 34 = 1987. Major market crash, probably related to program trading. (Remember that one?)

1953 + 55 = 2008. Major market crash and near-collapse of the global financial system because of the subprime mortgage mess.

How's them apples? (What happens in 2042, I wonder, which is 1953 + 89?) The market tops have progressed in increasing levels of seriousness. In 1958, we saw a deep recession, but it was not catastrophically serious. In 1966, we saw a substantial long-term top, and in 1974 the top and subsequent decline were even more so.

In 1987, this was still deeper, as the new derivatives and program trading nearly shattered everything. It may have been, in retrospect, some sort of warning about leveraging the banking and financial systems as was then being done. As usual, when impossibly large sums of money are being played with via trading games, this warning (as soon as the immediate dangers had passed) was completely ignored.

The entire financial industry nearly collapsed in 2008 with the subprime fiasco (and may yet do so, as the knock-on effects are still being felt). Therefore, if we make it to 2042, the system probably will collapse so badly that there will not be any real hope of restoring this Wall Street money machine to its former glory ever again. It will probably be that serious, if anybody wishes to place bets that far in advance!

Finally, I do not know if I was guided in some manner to discover all of these things both in this series of essays and from last year. I am not doing this for self-glorification but with a sense of strong humility. If I have been shown the way, then I give thanks to Him who took the time to point all of these things out to me.

My sense now tells me that I am unlikely to find any more interesting bits of future history related to pi and Fibonacci. Therefore, to my readers, just have a look at all of this from now and last year and just think and ponder what it could all mean. I believe the math is not to be refuted, so what *do* all of these cycles have to say? Is it all so gloomy?

So is it indeed all so gloomy? I am so very sorry to tell you that it is indeed, and probably much more. How can this be? Well, the underlying idea of this book is that we are living in the end times. What is this period, and why is it so significant? The books of the Bible have spoken of this many, many times. In essence, mankind is to experience something *really* dreadful that will repay us for all of the wickedness committed throughout our history.

We can say that it is a time when "the sins of the father will be visited upon the son" (Exodus 34:7). Some have spoken of this as a washing of the immense karmic debts under which we are all laboring. These are individual debts, but also national debts that have covered the whole world in iniquity.

The retribution will be so severe that Christ himself told his disciples on the Mount of Olives just before he was arrested that no flesh would be saved. The total destruction would be so intense that if it were not for the Elect, there would be nothing left at all. We are in that much trouble!

So, with this in mind and the fact that the Lord has said (millennia ago, so it is all planned out) mankind has to suffer in general, our period of history today seems to be the first real chance to exact holy retribution. Our world is linked, hand and foot, to the power of the US economy and the US dollar. Therefore, if there is to be "payback" for all that has been done wrong, it seems plausible that this will be accomplished in our generation and probably will start in the very near future.

This is what Fibonacci and pi have to say about all of this, and being a money professional, I am inclined to agree. In any event, as you have seen from what has been written already, we have the war cycle this year to start things off with the proverbial bang, and then at the end of next year the financial unraveling will hit hard.

After this, with confidence in the scores of trillions of dollars in global debt badly damaged, I do not see any realistic way of stopping this freight train. As confidence is a difficult, if not impossible, item to regain once lost, things will slide from bad to worse very quickly indeed. The end-times scenario is quite valid, in my sorry view.

Now what happens next? Can we measure this by our Fibonacci and pi methods? Yes, regrettably we can. Now I must talk to you about some more measurements which come from the book of Revelation and also tie in with what I have been writing.

Let us look at the seventh seal. Revelation states that "there was silence in heaven for the space of about half an hour" (Revelation 8:1). Given that we are looking at the best part of two thousand years between today and when St. John was informed of what must have been nearly unintelligible things (to him, anyhow), why would a major item such as the seventh seal deal with a tiny amount of time like half an hour?

What I believe is that one day in heaven is one thousand years "down here," as is written elsewhere in the Bible. If we extrapolate the half-hour from this ratio, we get that half an hour in heaven is equal to about 20.8 years down here.

I note that the time quoted is about half an hour, so if we extend the 20.8 years to 22 years, we are now at 31–32 minutes, which is certainly fitting the "about" time measurement (in heaven time, of course). We can also note that this time "down here" of 22 years fits in very nicely with events that the Fibonacci and pi timelines are suggesting. Let's see how, shall we? (Please recall my comments about the number 69 earlier on, and how 69, pi, and 22 all seem to be fairly closely interlinked.)

Twenty-two is a pi number (virtually exactly). That fits. I was also wondering about the "times, time, and half a time" (3.5 years) and how that ties in with things. Well, $22 = 7 \times 3.1416$, and I note that seven seems to crop up a lot in the Bible. Therefore, making the simple arithmetic adjustment, we see that 3.5 times pi is 11, again virtually exactly. Keep these numbers in mind.

My greatest fear after a bond market upheaval is that there will be political instability in Washington. If one can remember the problems we had during the debt ceiling crisis in October and November of last year, it is not beyond the realm of possibility that this may occur again—with even more force and uncertainty.

In looking at various Fibonacci and pi possibilities (and these include the numbers I have just mentioned—the "half an hour" numbers), we see that we start, as usual, with America's founding year—1776. We add 233 to this to bring us to 2009. Onto this we can now add 11 years, which seems reasonable as the 3.5 is mentioned quite often in Revelation. This brings us to the year 2020.

We can also arrive at this year by taking the war cycle years of 2014/15 and adding twice pi to this. (Remember the two times pi from Daniel, which I wondered if we would see anywhere else? We do!) We come to 2020 this way, as well.

Finally, Armstrong in some of his amazing charts sees that 2020 is also a target year, but this is derived from his economic cycles. So we can say US political instability arises from an economic base, which makes very good sense given where we are today and where we might very well be after the bond-market debacle on October 15, 2015.

As an interesting aside here, Armstrong mentions the year 2020 but refines it to 2,020.05. So if we now take 643 times pi, we also get 2020.05 exactly. Something is very definitely brewing at about this time, but what?

Let us look at a highly respected and venerated document: the US Constitution. It is an amazing piece of work that laid the foundation for the rise to global preeminence of a group of squabbling colonists in about two centuries. This is incredible, but what is its future? I read that a majority of states have ratified a Constitutional Convention to revise portions that might today be deemed obsolete.

Change is in the wind, but what does pi say? Well, we have looked at the year 2020 (or 2020.05), which says something, to be sure, but what else? The founding year of 1776 + 233 gives (as previously stated) 2009. As also noted, if one adds 11 on to this, we arrive at 2020. However, the US Constitution was promulgated in 1787, and if we go forward 233 years from this date we arrive at (drumroll, please) … 2020! Something *very* big regarding this document is in the wind.

One of the things Americans hold dear is the office of the presidency. Some forty-four people have held the office of the president, with Barack Obama being the most recent. Wait … no. There are only forty-three people if you count them one by one, as Grover Cleveland was both the twenty-second and twenty-fourth president, which muddies things a little bit.

If you look at the pi calculations I noted above, we see that the square root less the fourth root is 177–133, or 44. Maybe I am reaching a bit here, but there is so much in the simple derivatives (to use a word which so many people find disgusting these days) from Daniel that perhaps we can continue to extrapolate some more: especially as all of this fits so well with the future of the US Constitution.

We are at the forty-third president (in reality), which means that as Mr. Obama must step down in early 2017, the next president—Hillary Clinton?—must be the forty-fourth. Would she be the first woman president, and possibly the last one of all? If there is a major change in the US Constitution in 2020 (i.e., just before the normally scheduled quadrennial election scheduled for that fall), then the 44 number from the pi cycle would be accurate.

So we have *another* indicator that something big is brewing in just a few years. If I had to guess about all of this, I would say that the very dangerous financial crisis that looks to be brewing as we head into the year 2016 (an election year to boot) will leave our economy, which is pretty well dependent on ever-larger amounts of credit, in desperate straits.

As I have mentioned in the newsletter, it may well be that an attempted takedown of the United States' existing power structure might be in the cards as well. Yes, this is all in the book of Revelation and, by and by, I shall get to it and detail what I think will happen—always assuming that pi and the end-times theory are correct.

Oh, yes. Future dates that fit into 2032 (which is a seminal year for Mr. Armstrong) can be derived from what I have written above and also in (yet again) another manner. Armstrong gives the clear implication that various economic cycles (e.g., the interest rate hikes by then fed chairman Paul Volcker in 1981 plus 51 gives 2032) can be extrapolated to arrive at 2032 and then 2037.

I have to concur with what he is saying, as US history going forward will be, in the main, one of economics and the unwinding of really horrendous derivative bubbles. Therefore, we go back to the secondary recession of 2010 and add the twenty-two-year "half an hour" cycle and we get ... 2032! So this fits as well. The 2037 number can be derived by taking the 2015 year (looming larger and ever more important) and adding 22 yet again: 2015 + 22= 2037. I find it amazing how all of these things simply keep coming together.

Oh, all right. Let's have one more bit of analysis, then. Let's look at an institution which has dominated the United

States for just over a hundred years—becoming what many regard as a very sinister Christmas present in the year 1913. Is this a most wicked group of people (the twelve members of the board of governors, only seven of whom can vote at any one time) who can do whatever they want, to what might be the obvious detriment of the American people?

I take no position on this, although I will discuss it, as does the book of Revelation. I will analyze it in depth in a later segment of this book. However, we have just had the fed's centenary this past Christmas, and what happens now? Well, six pi cycles come to 18.85 years, and if one adds these to Christmas 2013, guess what we come up with?

Yep, it is our new friend, the year 2032. So do we have a terrible problem with the economy (possibly with the cashless society, which is also coming quite soon now—yes, Revelation again), which leads some desperate reformers to abolish what many people regard as a most venal institution? I think it quite probable.

So, within the now nailed-down parameters of 2010 and 2032, we shall clearly in the fullness of time be able to see smaller, but no less significant, subcycles. The major one, as far as I am concerned, lies in the interpretation of Revelation chapter 12 and the "war in heaven" analysis that I was making an informed guess about in the newsletter.

This is led by what appears to be conservative Christians, and we have to wonder about the US Constitution if this uprising takes place. Well, the founding document was written in 1787, and if we add the now-familiar 233 to this, we arrive at the year 2020. This, interestingly enough, is an exact pi cycle number as noted, and so I feel reasonably confident that it has a great deal of merit in pi cycle analysis in general.

So what I am saying is that this venerable US document will probably be changed either slightly by the winning side in the initial rebellion, or rather dramatically when the beast and its minions recapture control of the United States.

Have I let the cat out of the bag? I probably have, but let's let you stew and ponder this one. The South shall rise again, indeed!

SEGMENT 2

CHAPTER 1

The United States Eyes Canada
(Munch, Munch ... Chomp, Chomp?)

We might wonder if there is enough Pepto-Bismol in the world to correct the sort of stomach distress such a meal would cause. In all seriousness, we can note that throughout its history, the United States has eyed Canada and its vast open spaces and immense natural resources.

Chief among these, initially, must be oil, as seen in the Alberta tar sands, which are supposed to hold some 1.75 trillion barrels of oil.[1] To put this in understandable terms, if all of this could be mined (probably an accurate way to describe how this resource is currently being exploited), it would probably supply the fuel demands for the entirety of North America for three centuries. If a much smaller portion of all of this could be extracted before it was deemed that

---

1   *Wikipedia,* s.v. "Oil sands," accessed Nov. 30, 2014, http://en.wikipedia. org/wiki/Oil_sands.

nothing more could be taken, we are still looking at meeting North American demands for the rest of this century.

Given that Saudi Arabia may well be running out of what can be extracted profitably (not to mention the military threats and so forth endemic in that region), Alberta is a gift from God. In passing, I should note that other estimates (which I have used in my newsletters on this subject) put the tar sands deposits at about equal to all of the remaining crude oil deposits (i.e., non—tar sands type of oil) in the rest of the world.

Any way you put it, there is a terrific supply of oil in the remote northern reaches of Alberta. At present writing, we can say that most of this resource should probably be headed toward the United States (and the Texas refineries) via the long-delayed Keystone XL pipeline at some point in the future. However, it is not, and with very real problems in the Middle East never seeming to go away (since the 1973 Arab-Israeli War and the ensuing embargo in 1974), it stands to reason that oil producers in the United States are already casting covetous eyes on Alberta.

Americans have long had the feeling (it was referred to as Manifest Destiny many years ago) that they had natural rights to the entire continent of North America. When I studied this at school (just about fifty years ago—so it really is not a new idea) I came to the conclusion that in the aftermath of the Revolutionary War, there was not a lot of good feeling in the new states toward Great Britain and the rest of its global empire.

As Canada (not yet to be a nation for many decades to come) was part of this empire, it was (I suppose) only natural to the new capital of Washington that some sort of vast nation comprising North America should come into being. However, the new United States probably had more than enough on its nascent plate without worrying about why inhabitants of Upper and Lower Canada did not shuck off the British crown and join up with the former colonies to the south.

This feeling has not gone away in the least in the past two hundred-odd years, and every now and again, somebody in the corridors of power in Washington gets it in their head that the ongoing economic demands for the oft-sputtering US economy would be much more easily addressed if the two major countries on this continent were joined.

I suppose that one cannot forget "little" Mexico, and in the arcane world of NAFTA, any sort of continent-wide land grab by its major partner must include Mexico. I wrote about this possibility in my newsletters in November 2013, and the fact that Hillary Clinton (in my mind, the leading candidate to assume the presidency in the 2016 elections) also seems to have this under consideration.

I have followed this woman ever since her husband, Bill Clinton, won election to this office in 1992. She is, in my mind, extraordinarily intelligent and seems to have a strong lust for power to accomplish her own objectives. My sense is that she grew up in an era (essentially my own) when women were regarded as little more than an appendage to their husbands and were treated as such.

Understand that I am not going to write on this particular sociological subject, as it falls outside the purview of this book, but I do note it in passing, and I am sure that Hillary wanted to do something about it. Well, if she wins in 2016 (and I believe that she will), then she will have reached the summit of what a US woman can aspire to and will govern accordingly. That would be for domestic politics, but she has shown that she has a strong aptitude for international politics in what Americans would regard as, to borrow an old Soviet term, the "Near Abroad": namely, Mexico and Canada.

Just to highlight what I wrote in the newsletters, Clinton has made strong reference to a new way that NAFTA would work together in a Clinton presidency. Latinos in Los Angeles, where she gave the speech, apparently loved hearing from her in any event, and there was no bad feedback from what she said.

In March this year, she made a visit to Calgary and said very little of consequence to an overflow audience there, but then there was the point everyone missed: why she was there at all. Keep in mind that she visited a city where Canadian Prime Minister Harper comes from (his federal riding is located there), and so does then Premier Alison Redford (before she resigned suddenly in a spending scandal). A neighboring district (my own actually) is called home by the leader of the Wildrose provincial opposition party, Danielle Smith.

In this Albertan city, we also find the headquarters of many Canadian oil companies. So Hillary, in her very intelligent way of feeling something out, has probably made some good contacts for her presumed time at 1600 Pennsylvania Avenue. She has a plan in mind for North America—of that I am certain.

The comment Clinton made in Los Angeles last November was in an article taken from the *Washington Post*.

Her speech there was partially to "promote what Clinton called 'a shared future' between the two nations."[2]

Now if we add this to her coming to Calgary, we can say that she definitely has something in mind for North America, and it clearly includes Canada. I am guessing here, but I think it says that she wants US industrial capability combined with lots of cheap Mexican labor, all powered by nearly limitless Canadian natural resources.

❖ ❖ ❖

Now let's have a look at what Clinton did (according to the newspapers up here) on her trip to Calgary. Here is what I sent out in my newsletter. The thinking is still quite valid, in my view:

> I have postponed writing on this woman (again) until after her visit to Calgary on March 6. It looks like I needn't have bothered, as she came to the Telus Centre in Calgary and spoke before 2,500 curious souls for all of twenty-four minutes. The major question for Albertans is what is going to happen in Washington (either before or after a President Clinton takes office) regarding the Keystone pipeline, which would take the tar-sands oil to Texas for refining and selling.

---

2   Matea Gold, "In L.A., Supporters of a 2016 Hillary Clinton Campaign Are Ready to Get on Board Early," *Washington Post,* Nov. 9, 2013, http://www.washingtonpost.com/politics/in-la-supporters-of-a-2016-hillary-clinton-run-ready-to-get-on-board-early/2013/11/09/0298483c-48bd-11e3-a196-3544a03c2351_story.html.

At least six times, our Alberta Premier (roughly equivalent of a US state governor) has visited Washington to plead her case for the Obama Administration to drop its opposition to this venture, and every time Alberta has come away empty-handed. It therefore seems clear that nothing is going to be done during the tenure of President Obama. All Hillary had to say at the Telus Centre was that there was a process going on and that she could not comment any further!

This was very disappointing for both Premier Redford and Albertans in general. As if to rub in the fact that she had little to say, she commented on the igloo building program at Calgary University (yes, it seems that there is one) and made reference that while she was a great friend of Canadians in general, she did not know much about Calgary.

Oh yes, she made the seemingly obligatory comments equating Russian President Putin to Adolph Hitler. In other words, she was careful to say nothing at all that could be used against her as she plods along toward what seems to be a certain victory as Democratic candidate for US president in 2016 (i.e., the Democratic Party "process"), and then to be a most formidable candidate in the general election.

It looks like she has GOP strategists worried, as all they can apparently come up with to counter her immense popularity is a series of questions about her age and general health. I seem to recall that at the start of Ronald Reagan's first term, similar worries were expressed by the Democrats. Well, what goes around comes around.

Back to Mrs. Clinton's Calgary visit, if I may. Surely she did not come to Calgary to compliment the local university's igloo building program! She may have come to see where a possible challenger, Ted Cruz, was born (which makes me wonder how the GOP is going to explain this one, given their insistence that Barack Obama is ineligible for the office he holds as he was supposedly born in Kenya).

As Mr. Cruz was born here, perhaps he has some supporters, and perhaps she wanted to see who they are and what sorts of threats they may represent to her. What she may actually have done—and this makes more sense, as she is a very clever planner—is meet the overall movers and shakers here. What movers and shakers, you ask?

Well, Calgary is the oil capital of the most important oil patch on the planet (yes, the tar sands count), and this is where oil movers and shakers hang out. So the real question is, whom did she see, visit, and talk to (make deals with?) before she made her vacuous speech on Thursday morning? Enquiring minds want to know!

So what can we glean from this meet-and-greet, behind-the-scenes supposition? I think Hillary knows full well about the overall situation in the world, from the prospects of both energy and food security. Keep in mind the vast Ukrainian grain-growing areas.

It seems clear (and I shall discuss this next week on a Ukrainian update, which one reader asked me to do) that she is being regularly updated on these two situations and is planning accordingly. She has already made comments to the Los Angeles Latino community (although this ethnic grouping was probably already in her pocket) about bringing the three NAFTA nations together, which are essentially code words for bringing into the United States a whole panoply of skills from Mexico.

This influx and consequent increase in US industrial production would be fueled by Canadian (Albertan) oil, as we have discussed previously. Her trip to Calgary is to line up Canadian oil magnates and also politicians. Keep in mind that Prime Minister Harper comes from a Calgary district and represents it in Parliament in Ottawa. Alberta Premier Redford also comes from the Calgary area, and so the number of influential people Hillary may have gotten to meet is quite substantial.

She plans well. Of that there can be no doubt. She was US Secretary of State and therefore knows a very great deal about how things are transacted around the world. The interesting question is whether she advised President Obama on what might happen in the Ukraine and how this could be moved to US advantage.

As an aside here, just how strong is the United States, anyhow? From what I am reading on RT.com, it seems that President Putin looks to be climbing down on the issue of Russians in the Eastern portion of the Ukraine concerning their security and may even be considering something similar in the Crimea.

I cannot believe this, to be frank, but the fact that he is doing next to nothing while the new ad-hoc government in Kiev is flexing its muscles is astonishing. Does Hillary know the man that well, and that when push comes to shove he can be told (in effect) what to do? Such a woman, as US president (especially when she has been recently described as a very tough person), would be a formidable opponent throughout the world.

There is, of course, the problem of getting by the US election process in 2016, but I suspect she is not unduly concerned. If she has had the opportunity to talk with oil moguls during her Calgary trip, then I would imagine it may be a fairly simple process to offer them "considerations" in return for their supporting what she has in mind for the period 2017–21 (at least).

Now, if she can do this to Albertan oil executives, then how much more pressure can she bring on US executives? My guess is that many Mexican workers, on goodness knows what sorts of visas, will come to the United States. What Hillary is probably telling these business interests is that, for them, the clear implication is that huge new profits can be reaped with lower fringe benefits (think health care here) at the very least.

Hillary would be a powerful incentive for these people to support her in 2016, and I am sure she knows all about this. Find their weak spot and hit at it. It will work well in the United States and almost certainly with the oil people in Alberta. Something along these lines is her probable plan, and while I do not like her, I must commend her ruthlessness in planning this far ahead.

So what now, assuming all of this supposition on my part is correct? Well, I am not a confidant of Mrs. Clinton, clearly, but I would look for more strategic planning depending on what goodies the US State Department can cook up (i.e., where is the next Ukraine?). She most probably has good contacts in that department and will use them unceasingly.

The GOP also knows all of this, and it might be behind the recent stories that Hillary is either "too old" to serve or has possible health problems, as referenced above. If this is the best they can do, there is little chance they will succeed in a little under three years against an opponent as formidable as Mrs. Clinton!

Well, have a look at all of this and be prepared (for right or wrong) for America's first woman president and its forty-fourth overall. She will be very calculating and exceptionally well informed, and she has a very good idea of what she wants to do because she has already worked it all out in that wonderful mind of hers!

I do not believe that she will be that relenting to her opponents (and the GOP may regret taking her on with various issues). In fact I would even go as far as to say that the GOP is probably wondering who they can put up as their candidate against her and are probably crying in their beer over the fact that she is a Democrat! Such is life in America's political capital.

However, she is but one cog in the wheel on the whole emotive subject of a United States/Canada merger (as it has been referred to in the newsletter). So let us assume that Hillary will be the forty-fourth president, which means she will be a prime mover (if not *the* prime mover) on this sorry subject. For there to be any movement at all on this, there must be an underlying base of economic fundamentals, or else nothing at all would be happening—and this chapter in the book would not even have been considered, much less written.

CHAPTER 2

Still Munching and Chomping (Who Else besides Hillary Has This Enormous Appetite?)

I spent almost the entirety of chapter 1 looking at the very dangerous, highly intelligent, and probably soon-to-be leader of the United States and how, I believe, she is looking at a takeover of Canada. Speaking as a Canadian, I am most concerned with how the wheels in her head will grind ever finer and finer as she becomes ever more at home in her new office in 2017.

However, that is roughly two and a half years from now. That is a long time in the forecasting business. Given that we still have a war cycle to stagger through (thank Marty Armstrong for this, unfortunately as accurate as ever), followed by a major bond-market debacle about eighteen months from now, there must be something that the United States-phobes in Canada have to be more concerned about. Regrettably, there is.

I should probably wait until this book's segment on oil before going into this more fully, but in order to let you see what I am worried about in terms of Canada's sovereignty, I had better explain the principle of "backwardation" now. This is very counterintuitive (typical of today's markets, I suppose), but it is accurate in any event. I shall leave aside the mathematics of time decay on prices and so forth and stick with the very basics.

Let us look at crude oil markets as we see them today, and which can be verified on the COMEX markets that trade in Chicago. Let us say the month that sees all of the action is June, and standard delivery crude is trading at $99.50 per forty-two US gallon barrel. Well, not all of the trading takes place in this front month (as it is called). Traders can hedge and speculate in a wide range of dates going out to December 2022, so it is quite a liquid market: what is called "deep."

Oil trades for a final settlement price (the final price, in other words) each trading day. The difference between the price quotes of, say, June and July is what interests us in looking at the phenomenon of backwardation. In the final analysis, this tells us a lot about the availability of crude and how this will affect Canada. Let me scream this out in no uncertain terms: A BACKWARDATED MARKET IS ONE THAT CALLS FOR *SHORTAGES* GOING FORWARD. THAT'S RIGHT—SHORTAGES AND *NOT* SURPLUSES! Okay, Gerry, you have made your point. Now what *does* this mean?

So we see the June contract price is $99.50, and backwardation price structure tells us that the July price is $99.00 (i.e., fifty cents *less* than the June price). Yes, you read that right. The July price is lower than the June price and, because this so-called backwardation goes all the way out to December 2022, we see the price there at $80.13, which is a *discount* of about 19.5 percent to June 2014. So why is this? Why is it that a commodity in short supply sees its price become cheaper in the future? At the very least such would seem to be counterintuitive, but that is the way it is. Again, *why is this so?*

All right, think along the following lines. If you believe, for whatever reason, that oil is in short supply, what do you do? Well, if I were an end user, I would make sure that I had all that I could handle. I would make sure that every storage container I possessed was full to the brim with real, useable product that I would have to sell to my customers.

This means that in the next few months, having the feeling that a shortage could be coming, I would buy some of my requirements for, say, the next six months today and store them immediately. This would have the effect of bidding up the contracts for the next few months at the expense of contracts for the end of the year or even over the next few years. Therefore, we would see the backwardation develop which we are seeing so extensively in the crude oil markets today. Again, backwardation is seen when the price of two monthly contracts, in our case June and July 2014, sees June at $99.50 and July at $99.00.

Buying, possibly made greater by overall fears of a gathering shortage, would be concentrated in the next few months at the expense of, say, Christmas contract. More buying now and less at Christmas means the price now will be higher than in the December (Christmas) contract.

We should also not forget the problem that in dealing with commodities, there is the storage factor. If everyone wants to buy now and hold the commodity until needed, this will also bid up the storage price, as this legitimate cost must be added to the final price for the consumer. Therefore, if you wish to buy now and avoid paying a hefty storage fee to someone who has bought a contract for July, or August, or whenever, you must compensate that person. We see this in the backwardated price curve (learning the lingo now, are we?).

So if you buy a contract for December 2022 with the intent of sitting on it for roughly eight and a half years, you will be compensated an amazing (as already noted) 19.5 percent for your costs. That is, of course, if you are a speculative player and say "Right! Oil is going *much* higher, and this is the cheapest I can get. I will buy and hold."

If oil went to $200 in December 2022, then you would sell your contract at $200 and make the spread that was available from today, plus 19.5 percent. You would be rich! Yes, you would be, assuming that the organized markets hold together long enough for your contract to mature and for you to take your healthy profits and run away to somewhere nice to live your life of ease.

We might also say with a 19.5 percent discount that perhaps the market is saying something like "Eight and a half years is a long time to wait for my profits. What happens if the rising oil price causes a really devastating recession, which would cause the price of oil to fall a very long way? It is likely that you will see something like this happen, so why are you taking such a huge risk?" The answer is that the market feels a 19.5 percent discount is probably about right for the risk you are taking.

However, that is all trader talk. This chapter is about a US takeover of Canada (which has been called "the merger" by myself and others), and so what can we say about the real purpose of this takeover? I say (and there must be a *lot* of people in official Washington think tanks agreeing with this) that with growing oil shortages (they ain't making the stuff anymore), the major consumers in the United States may be sick of all of the machinations in the Middle East. They want stability in their sources of supply.

Let me put this all as plainly as I can. Backwardation means shortages of crude going forward as we have seen. *The United States is short of oil. Canada (Alberta) has plenty of the stuff. The United States needs this. It will try to get it via a giant Canada/United States merger, is my argument.*

They, the US consumers, note that Britain and Argentina are at loggerheads over what could be an enormous find in the remote Falkland Islands. Britain is so anxious to hang onto this (the Falklands being a British colony and voting by a very wide margin to retain this status in a referendum about a year ago) that London is building a major airstrip on the very remote island of St. Helena, which could be used, at short notice, to fly military equipment to the Mt. Pleasant airbase in the Falklands. St. Helena is also a British colony.

We can see also that China is gazing, eyeball to eyeball, with the Philippines, Vietnam, and Japan over various claims in the huge South China Sea. While I have not heard that much about this in the last little while, oil (what else?) was mentioned as a prime motivator for all of this possible hostility.

There is much aggravation in the world over oil, so does it not make sense that people at the head of Exxon and the like would much appreciate a breather from all of it? And look at nice, quiet Canada (and Alberta in particular)!

And this is what I have been leading up to. Canada (and Alberta in particular, which has just about all of the continent's tar sands deposits) is a nice quiet place where nothing ever seems to happen.

The quasi-separatist portion of Canada is located in Quebec and is thousands of miles away. In contrast, quiet Alberta has a pro-business attitude and a flat tax that everyone on the continent seems to envy. Surely if the US oil majors wanted an easy set of oil production quotas, then this would be the place.

What I think happened is that a lot of people, looking at the mess of global oil supplies (rapidly contracting, as can be seen in the backwardation phenomenon), decided that a Canada/United States merger was definitely in the interests of Washington's energy planning. So, given this, we came to a story in the *Washington Times*.

There was an interesting comment earlier this year in the *Washington Times*, which tends to be somewhat to the right of center in US political discourse, as I understand it. It ran what I think has to be what is referred to as a "merger" trial balloon in the form of an article from the Canadian equivalent publication, the *National Post*.

The story, which was not well put together regarding facts and the like, was all about how the United States and Canada should finally come together as one political unit under one flag in North America. I wrote on this merger idea in the newsletter at some length and I wish to include this now. It reads:

> No, I am not referring to some sort of mega-corporate get-together, but rather something I have noted in the past and which is rearing its ugly head once again: a possible takeover of Canada by the United States. This seems to come to the fore every few years, and now it might even be some sort of political takeover by neocons or a play for the biggest oil reserves on the planet: the Alberta tar sands.
>
> I have written about the possibilities of Alberta and British Columbia looking to go it alone if there were real problems stirring in Ottawa (Canada's capital) over energy mining, for that is how the tar sands are effectively developed. In that essay, I wondered about the US authorities allowing such a conglomerate to exist for anything but a short period of time.
>
> Since I wrote that series of updates, we have seen (and heard on Slovak radio) some very good comments by the redoubtable Paul Craig Roberts to the effect that the neocons pretty well control the decision-making process in Washington and that their goal is total global hegemony, where their word is essentially global law.
>
> To get this operation into full swing, Washington would have to have access to unlimited amounts

of energy. This would be required to ensure that Washington could do whatever it wanted on a global scale (probably militarily) with no worries about this critical energy component.

As Washington grabbed more and more resources on its apparent never-ending hunt, the rest of the world would be squeezed badly— think China here. So am I having some sort of nightmare as I write this? No, I do not think so. Have a look at the following.

At about the same time that Mr. Roberts was making his comments about the sheer evil that seems to be running Washington, we see an article trotted out in a rather right-wing newspaper called "Border Buddies: A Merger Between the United States and Canada?" with a subheadline reading, "Visionary Writer Starts with a 'Thought Experiment.'"[3]

It smells to me like the proverbial trial balloon. If we examine some of the comments in the article, we also see that it would be a resource grab of the largest dimension imaginable. For example: "'I wanted to attack the Canadian establishment and say, "Wake up, there is [a merger] underway,

---

3   Meghan Drake, "Border Buddies: A Merger Between the United States and Canada?" *Washington Times,* March 23, 2014, http://www.washingtontimes.com/news/2014/mar/23/border-buddies-author-touts-merger-between-the-uni.

let's manage it to our benefit," and to attack American ignorance about Canada,' she said."

Note the words, "Wake up, there is a merger underway." Further on in the article, we see: "The North American colossus would control more oil, water, arable land and resources than any other country, all protected by the world's most powerful military."

And we have (as this newspaper article is written by a Canadian who apparently contributes to the *National Post* in Canada) something from an American writing for a foreign policy journal called *Suffragio*: "Kevin Lees, founder and editor of the foreign policy journal *Suffragio*, said the United States can benefit easily and immediately from 'low-hanging fruit' in Canada."

So if we take all of these things together, we see a resource grab. The three comments noted above talk about "a merger being underway"; "more oil, land, and water than anybody else"; and "low-hanging fruit." If I have misinterpreted all of this, hopefully the reader will forgive me. But if it walks like a duck and quacks like a duck, then it probably is a duck! Let's come back to this resource angle a little later on.

If we reread the story from the *Washington Times*, we see that a merger would reportedly add thirteen stars to the US flag, as this number of provinces would become states. Well, Canada does not have thirteen provinces. It has ten provinces and three territories: the Yukon, Northwest Territories, and Nunavut.

To just take one of these, the Yukon (which I happen to be familiar with), we see that it has about 33,000 people living there, about 75 percent of which are in the territorial capital of Whitehorse. The territory is about 186,000 square miles in area, which would make it appreciably larger than most US states.

Still, I do not see a huge land area, mostly uninhabited, being admitted to the United States as a state with only 33,000 people. Not many people live "up north" in Canada as a whole, and to create three new states from ice and snow is not going to work at all.

However, the author seems to think this will be the case, even though she wishes to consign Canada's problem child of Quebec to the status of Puerto Rico: a territory. So the author wishes to deprive nearly eight million Canadian citizens of the right to vote, as well as representation in a Congress in Washington, on the basis of ethnicity while allowing a few score thousand to have full such rights (which other US flyweights, such as Guam, do not).

Wonderful thinking, and if the rest of what she writes about is of the same quality, then perhaps we could end this lengthy essay here and now! Look at her math. There are (she says, as noted) thirteen provinces (ten, in reality) which will obtain stars on the revised US flag. But with only nine provinces in her math (i.e., the ten we have now less Quebec makes nine), I wonder about the author.

However, she did us a service in addressing this issue. The US authorities have shown themselves to be most amenable to a takeover of Canada, most recently in terms of trade benefits for both sides.

In the late 1950s, when the United States was rapidly expanding its economy after WWII, there was an initiative called NAWAPA, short for North American Water And Power Alliance. Basically, for the large amount (for back then, with the rather limited capital markets versus what we have today) of $100 billion, the United States wanted to make Canada what would have been the ultimate hewer of wood and drawer of water.

The interior of British Columbia was to be filled with what would have been a giant lake for US irrigation purposes and possibly a reserve for western hydroelectric dams. Northern Quebec was to be a huge supplier of hydropower for the industrial US northeast, and on and on it went. Mercifully, nothing came of this—I am guessing because of the estimated expense. Still, it gave us an indication of what the thinking was in the corridors of power in Washington.

Not much else was done on this issue until the middle to late 1960s, when the issue rose again. Then we saw the idea of a commonality of interests, which would have resulted in Washington enticing the western provinces (excluding BC, for some reason) into the United States, with all of the staggering resources available.

Ontario was left out of this equation, despite its industrial capacity, which laid bare the idea of a raw materials grab. At that time, interestingly enough, Quebec did not seem to figure in Washington's economic calculus, and on the maps of the proposed new North America it was marked either independent or other. Again, with the general disgust over the Vietnam conflict, nothing came of this.

The United States is now trying the NAFTA idea to rope Canada and Mexico into the proposed North American

Union, and at one point maybe ten years ago we had President Bush come up with the idea of a common North American currency, somewhat lamely called the Amero.

The way this was to be set up was little better than a scam of immense proportions, and when this became generally realized, the idea was dropped. However, I am getting ahead of myself a bit here. In 1990, the Quebec issue and the infamous Meech Lake Accord reared its ugly head in Canada once again. And once more, I started to see syndicated editorials in major US newspapers about how the United States could absorb Canada.

This time, we were looking at blocs of provinces that would be absorbed into a common union. BC would form one state, the Prairie Provinces would form another, Ontario and then Quebec would be two others (no leaving Quebec out this time, given the extraordinary importance of hydropower to the northeastern States)—and then no one could figure out what to do with Canada's welfare provinces "down east." This also went nowhere fast, and I never saw it raised again, at least in this format.

Now we see the latest incarnation of the merger idea. It is, again, a play for natural resources, and this might finally see all of the marbles on the table. Unlike the days of NAWAPA and other attempts, there are things which the now-developed financial markets are telling us about energy supplies going forward—globally this time.

I have written about all of what follows before, but I wish to do so again as I desire, strongly, to emphasize the global positioning in oil. Again, we note that COMEX is seeing a backwardation of prices for as far out as one cares to go. (Mercifully, it does not seem to be growing, although

I am worried when I see a near-term widening of this critical measure.)

In terms of tradable contracts, we can go to 2022 and still see the stubborn message that oil is in short supply (relative to increasing global demand), and this is not going to change one iota. One new thing I can add here is the degree of demand from US trading houses.

As a former trader speaking here, I can say that there is one thing I pay the strictest attention to, and that is market bias. Recently, certain events should have spelled that there was, for the short term at least, an oversupply of oil that should have pushed the price down fairly sharply.

The biggest of these was the ongoing belief that the Chinese economy (which is the second biggest user of oil in the world after, of course, the United States) was weakening, possibly dramatically so. Under normal circumstances, this should have seen a large crude selloff, but not this time. The spot price fell from $103.00 to $97.50 or so and then bounced dramatically to recoup nearly all of this. We are told that there was a big demand for West Texas Intermediate (WTI, a.k.a., light sweet crude oil, a grade of crude oil used as a benchmark in oil pricing), and whereas this is worth knowing as the reason for the bounce, it is still only one part of the equation for oil pricing.

A major slowdown in China would mean a sustained drop in prices because a lot of oil that used to go to China would be without a home (translation—would be sold on the futures markets at a discount). The China story should have been enduring, as it is *huge*, and yet the Cushing supply for WTI seemed to rule the roost.

In short, whenever there is a dip in oil prices for whatever reason, a *lot* of buyers suddenly come into focus. The bias is therefore for oil to be actively sought after, whatever the news and possible changes are and how they affect macro considerations.

The demand from sources which actually use the stuff is strong, and this does not include trading houses and banks (keep in mind the trader known as "God," whom I believe is still around—see the end of the book), which will have noticed the price bias and actively be on the bids as prices see occasional falls. Let me emphasize this. Backwardation says that there are shortages for as far out as you care to go. This is serious for a major consumer such as the United States.

Price bias says that there are *lots* of fresh buyers at virtually every major price level. Why on earth should you *not* be a buyer, given these considerations, either speculatively or for "real" purposes? Speaking as a trader, you should, and we shall continue to see this idea, I think. Now that I have been writing on this, let me draw it all into the theme for this series of letters: a Canada/United States merger.

The redoubtable Paul Craig Roberts has been writing and giving radio interviews about how the very right-wing neocons have taken power in Washington behind the scenes and, no matter who is temporarily in the White House, their agenda is the only one that matters. Roberts says that they want nothing less than American hegemony across the globe and are so determined to have this for what he calls "the exceptional people" that they are risking nuclear war with Russia—which they believe is winnable.

Okay, so much for the political aspects of what Washington, DC, may or may not want. The idea I have is that in order to gain this global supremacy the United States must have unfettered access to a full set of industrial components, such as hydroelectric power, raw materials, and of course oil. According to Wikipedia, the tar sands (yep, back to that again) has as much oil as the rest of the world has in conventional reserves: some 1.6 trillion barrels.

For an avaricious oil major, this is a prize of world-beating proportions and must be secured before it may be sold off to Chinese interests or—heaven forbid—the energy-starved EU which, be it remembered, is trying to conclude a trade pact with Canada (the long-delayed CETA accord). Neocons would desire this treasure, and they would want it before a CETA-inspired Shell Oil Company (as an example) grabs a portion of it. It seems to be a question of control.

So with all of the cards now in the process of being laid on the table, we see that global demand for energy, in the face of ever-expanding industrial production, is now going to soar. Longer-term planners will have noticed this, and we see that Manitoba and BC hydros will be a very important component of what Washington feels the level of US economy should be performing at.

The question is how to access this, as it would take a pliant government in Ottawa to be able to get this done. My guess is, with federal elections scheduled for next year in Canada, that the neocons would want a Conservative government (such as the one we have today under Prime Minister Harper) that could be pressured into presenting something along these lines to the Canadian public.

If Washington were to wait too long, then we might have a Liberal government under Justin Trudeau, the son of the late popular Pierre Elliot Trudeau, who ruled the roost as

PM for many years starting in 1968. Justin's Liberals have a decent lead over Harper at present, and I do not believe that as a new PM (should he win next year) he would like to make a monumental decision such as the merger, at least not immediately.

Remembering his father as I do, we might say that Justin would not like the idea anyhow. So, with time short in my estimation, Washington has to act.

Again, referring back to the newsletter:

> If we consider again the *Washington Times* article, a couple of lines stand out for me. It noted that in the US foreign policy journal *Suffragio*, we see a very blunt comment: "'The good news is that policymakers on both sides of the border are very much considering those ideas,' he said."

> So was there some really strong talk at the recent NAFTA summit in Mexico then? If *Suffragio* makes this sort of very unambiguous comment, then I am inclined to think that there was. Following this summit and the comments about neocon supremacy in Washington, an article such as what we are seeing, backed up with a lot of behind-the-scenes comments, is probably the next step in this most audacious plan.

> Will Harper go along with this at all, knowing that it would not be popular across the country? If he is looking to leave some sort of legacy, then he might, knowing full well that there would not be the force in Parliament to counter his wishes,

although there would probably be some nasty infighting on the entire issue in his Cabinet.

What Harper will probably have to do is to have some sort of continent-wide decision-making authority with this grouping approved within Canada, so that the border (in theory at least) still remains intact. This would provide a fig leaf for Liberal and NDP supporters (Canada's major opposition parties) to claim that nothing really has changed.

We could still see a Canadian dollar in use (much as several countries in the EU still use their own currencies—Sweden, Denmark, the UK, and Poland come to mind) in an expanded North American condominium such as what we are discussing. That too would be for show, and it would be kept in a very tight band in trading against the powerful US dollar.

All right, we have looked at oil to the point of exhaustion, but there is another element we have to have a quick look at, and that is water. Canada has huge reserves of this most precious resource, most of it locked away in the remote territories of Nunavut and the NWT.

Under the terms of NAFTA, US interests cannot get at this water unless Canada declares it to be a commodity that can be exploited fully within the country. Then US interests can claim that under the trade treaty, they have a perfect right to climb on board this particular gravy train and exploit it to a fare-thee-well.

It is probably this fear that has kept water away from parched states, as there is still a very strong belief that the United States has squandered its own very substantial resources in this area. And why should the United States be given access to anything more to waste yet again?

We must examine this belief, and I think that it might be very well behind what the neocons are trying to accomplish. A United States/Canada under NAFTA means that Canada's water is safe despite more and more grumbling about how the US farm belt, especially under the dubious heading of global warming, needs this water urgently.

A Canada that is part of the United States to the extent of having its own stars on the US flag would be quite a different matter. As a single country, the water would be up for grabs. In some respects, one can see that a long-term thinking neocon would be saying that, by and large (with CETA exceptions noted briefly above), the United States can get the oil it needs from Canada when it wants it.

It is only the political control that is missing. However, what is the point of having all of the oil one can ever use if the means to grow crops in the United States is to be impaired? Therefore, if the idea of having an economically solid US economy is at the base of overseas expansion, the water situation *must* be taken care of. It must also be eliminated as a worry as soon as possible, in my view, especially with all of the headlines about a five-hundred-year drought in California being bandied about.

Well, let's close off this rather lengthy series on an event that may never come to pass. (Perhaps the United States undergoes financial collapse—not impossible, given the pi and Armstrong analyses—before it can make eyes at Canada, however that is done these days!) What do I think of all of this? Do I approve?

No, manifestly I do not, as there are simply too many negatives for Canada in such an arrangement. If you wish, it is an agreement between two partners who are *not* equal. Where is the benefit for Canadians? Do they get to go and live in retirement in Arizona without any visa nonsense? (Wow! What's that really worth anyway?)

Do they get (depending on where they live, of course) to send representatives to Washington's Congress, where they will be dwarfed by the large number of Congressmen from US states by probably a 9:1 ratio? Would they adopt the

IRS Tax Code? Definitely I would ask, "Where's the benefit?"

I also worry about Medicare (being an official senior citizen now). It is self-funding in Alberta because of the huge oil revenues, but what happens after a takeover? Are oldies like myself to be grandfathered in? I can probably go on and on with this, as you can imagine, but to what extent?

If people like those in DC (who most probably want this sort of thing to occur) have their eyes set on money and power and how fast it can be accumulated, then they will not give the proverbial tinker's damn about the annoying complications which will be sure to arise. Devil take the hindmost indeed! Do I approve of such a merger?

As stated before, I certainly do *not*. However, that being said, will it happen? With deep regret, I believe that it will. How can I say that? Simply this: look at how a trader would regard everything I have presented. A good trader will assess the trend overall and go with it. From the days of NAWAPA to today's resource-starved world, this trend is getting stronger. Therefore (shudder) it *will* happen, and probably a lot sooner then people think.

Think on this, especially my Canadian readers.

It is a play for oil; of that there is no question. We must also keep in mind that there is something else I alluded to briefly, and that is fresh water. This is *so* important that I wish, again, to reemphasize it. The United States is running into problems here with their insistence that domestic supply will never run dry and that rich builders can become ever richer by raising new cities in desert areas like Arizona and Nevada.

Great golf courses are being constructed as well, and there never seems to be a concern as to how the populations here will be able to obtain the ever-growing supplies of water to make this all work. Even the recent headlines about California looking at poor levels in reservoirs and a possible five-hundred-year drought have not dissuaded the profit-crazed developers.

In fact, recently I saw a projection that California by the year 2030 might be looking at a population of perhaps forty million people. This is considerably more than the entire population of Canada today! What irritates me is the incessant desire to grow and build at all costs (and with the possible arrival of millions of new immigrants, this is probably preordained) with no thought as to how to make it work.

So the people with say-so in the United States will be looking at Albertan oil, to be sure, but also the immense reserves of fresh water to be found in the Northwest Territories and Nunavut. It is probably the water that will tip the scales when all is said and done.

Canada has about 20 percent of the world's fresh water reserves, more than any other country. It is a prize worth coveting, in other words. Given global growth and shortages in North America, this is where the deal for the merger will probably go through.

Finally, let me look at another trial balloon being floated here regarding the merger. A major Canadian business paper has climbed onboard this particular bandwagon in recent months and feels that when all of the assets of a united United States/Canada were taken into consideration, every Canadian would be entitled to a lump-sum payment of about $500,000.

Basing this on a German model for their reunification in 1990, it would probably be calculated on years of residency, and the actual payout would be factored in over at least two decades. If you think about it, if you were given $500,000 in one lump sum, what would you do? Well, all that nasty credit card debt would be gone in a flash—and maybe a nice new house?

Well, what would happen to the price of those houses with everyone trying to buy at the same time? What would happen to the price of cars, or the price of anything else for that matter? The West German payout to the old East Germany was well absorbed, and there is no reason (according to this article) why a payment to Canadians could not be managed in a similar manner.

Lots in this chapter, to be sure, for you to assess and analyze. What about other ways that Americans could stick their claws into the parts of Canada that really matter? (You can tell where I stand on this issue, can't you?) Well, there is another major possibility, and we shall discuss this in our next chapter.

CHAPTER 3

The Future of Western Canada—Could Washington Let It Survive as an Independent Entity? (Is This as Simple as ABC?)

All kidding aside, the ABC referred to in the title is that of a new country—Alberta/British Columbia—made up of the names of the current two westernmost provinces in Canada. I am sure you are amazed that I would even consider such a thing, but I am very serious. Think back to the last chapter, when I made a brief reference to this possibility. Now let me spell it all out for you.

As a western Canadian, with my home province being Alberta, I have seen many things that show me that the bonds between Ottawa (back east) and Edmonton (our provincial capital) are not as strong as many would think. A few months ago, I wrote a series of newsletters on this possibly contentious subject, and these will form the backbone of this chapter. I have reviewed them (clearly) and am quite happy with the information in them.

I will mention before I enclose them that what follows is probably a reasonable follow-on from the merger comments of chapter 2. There the underlying theme was of a merger between nonequals, with the possibility of some sort of payout to Canadians for the indignity of having the United States/NAFTA taking Canada away from the ranks of the independent nations of the world.

In this chapter, we are considering something completely different. I am wondering about the possibility of some sort of secession by the two western provinces of Alberta and British Columbia. Strictly from a cash-flow perspective, this would be a nasty blow to the economic strength of central Canada, where most of the nation's population resides.

However, please be good enough to read what I wrote a few months ago on this subject, below. Then, I wish to close with how all this plays into a US desire (let us say a desperate and burning desire) to grab what is available for its withering supply of critical raw materials. If they are on the same continent, raw materials have to be a major priority for Washington these days, in whatever form is contemplated.

Here are my newsletter comments from a few months ago:

> Perhaps I am drifting off into the realms of never-never land, but in reviewing very old files, I came across an oddity that merits more attention these days, in my view. My persistent gaze upon this subject involves a possible separation of the provinces of Alberta and British Columbia from

the rest of Canada proper. After your jaw has finished dropping somewhat on reading this, let me tell you my tale.

About ten years ago, I was a farmer in northern Alberta struggling to stay afloat financially, even though the rest of the province was making enormous amounts of money from its massive energy resources. In fact, it was making so much money that the rest of Canada was starting to complain, and the minority federal government of Paul Martin (coincidentally my MP when we used to live in the Quebec riding of LaSalle) started to take notice.

There was the usual bantering back and forth between Martin's government and its provincial counterpart under the conservative firebrand, Ralph Klein. Nothing really happened until Martin, a veteran of the days of Pierre Elliot Trudeau and his National Energy Programme (NEP), decided to step up the pressure and mentioned the possibility of revisiting this with some sort of price controls on Alberta oil, either directly or indirectly (through taxation).

The resulting fury could be seen in one of the daily polls published by the *Edmonton Journal* as to whether Alberta should separate because of a Liberal government in Ottawa, when there was no Alberta representation in any form in this administration. The poll results showed the separation idea losing, but only by 49–50 percent, which told me a great deal.

I suppose that Martin saw this, as well, because he telephoned Klein from a visit to the Northwest Territories, and great was the federal comedown! No more did we hear anything about price controls to cover the cost of petroleum products, although Klein did his part by reducing the huge provincial fiscal surplus.

I can still recall the way this was done. I had been applying for some sort of farming grant to tide me over, and the telephone rang one day on the farm to tell me that it had all been approved. What happened next I shall always recall. The young lady in the provincial treasury asked me, "By the way, is there any other grant or subsidy we can approve for you?" In all honesty there wasn't, and I told her so, to her apparent disappointment. Mr. Klein made sure that his surplus was reduced with great speed. The trouble between Ottawa and Edmonton vanished very quickly after all of this.

Alberta is *very* defensive about its natural resources (which it owns under the Canadian Constitution), and so I wondered about what happens today. The last Liberal federal MP elected in Alberta was way back in 1968, during the days of Trudeaumania and the sweep by the then Prime Minister Pierre Trudeau, in that year's election. His party, the Liberal Party of Canada, is detested in Alberta and has paid the price for the National Energy Policy and other apparently anti-Alberta measures for nearly fifty years now. There is to be an election by 2015, and the current Harper Administration (Conservative, with Mr. Harper's riding located in Calgary, Alberta) is not favored to win, looking at polls today.

The Liberal Party currently seems to have been enjoying some sort of renaissance in populous eastern Canada and is headed by none other than the son of Mr. Trudeau, who was famous in the 1960s, '70s, and '80s. Could we therefore see a replay of what he sought to achieve back then?

Could the energy situation be such that some sort of possibly illegal pressure from Ottawa on Alberta's oil and its production (think tar sands) might be forthcoming after the next election, if the new Trudeau wins a majority or even a working minority in conjunction with the social democrat party, the New Democrats? In my view, it is possible, and now I have to explain all of this to you and what the implications might be.

In preparing this essay, my thinking was that we might be looking at some sort of growing oil shortage in the world (see my comments over the past several months about growing backwardation on the COMEX in oil prices). As such, the price of tar-sands oil could very well spike higher, thus generating huge windfall accruals for the Provincial Treasury in Edmonton.

This would be at the clear expense of heavily populated Ontario, where the current version of Mr. Trudeau must do well if he is to have any hope of forming a government next year. I think you can see where I was thinking of going with this, given what his father did with the NEP in the early 1980s. If this idea is correct, then a left-of-center government in Ottawa (replacing that of Mr. Harper) would certainly look at fixing the price (and hence profit levels).

I am sure the Chinese would love that, what with their $15 billion purchase of Nexen just under a year ago—all or most of this going up the proverbial spout for the benefit of central Canadians. However, things (upon deeper reflection) have changed since 1980.

People are now concerned about the environment, and the ongoing worry about global warming is simply not going away. Personally, I do not believe in this theory (call it what it is, I suppose) and think that we are seeing swings in global temperatures that would be consistent with global cooling over a long-term basis. I recall all of this so well from the late 1970s, when various scientists started talking about the possibility of a summer coming where the snow from the previous winter would not melt.

However, what I think is irrelevant in the grand scheme of things, and as of now the powers that be seem to be considering that the exceptionally cold winter in North America in 2013–14 is consistent with the dreaded global warming. Certainly, US President Barack Obama has mandated that at the federal level, global warming is official policy.

Enduring the butt of all sorts of jokes that if we have much more of the current version of global warming we shall all freeze to death, he is sticking to what he believes. Given the enormous financial and economic power of the United States, no one can ignore what he is saying—especially with nearly three years in his term of office remaining. It was this thought that persuaded me to change what I had originally intended to write.

I would think that the global-warming crowd is well positioned. A massive drought in California, which is estimated to be as bad as anything in the past five hundred years, is laid at the doorstep of a high-pressure cell over southern

California that will simply not be dislodged for any appreciable period of time.

It would not be hard for environmentalists to state that the extreme hot, dry weather in California is a function of global warming and that we have to make serious changes to what we, as North Americans, do—literally *today*. I am also reading that, excluding the horrendous North American winter in 2013–14, the world is slightly warmer today than it was over the past few years.

Mankind seems to know so little about the complex interactions as to how ocean currents and temperatures moderate or intensify various trends, but that means little: global warming must be faced and combated, and the sooner the better (i.e., *now*). So where does that leave us with our probable showdown between Ottawa and Canada's two western provinces?

The Green Party in Canada is not that popular in terms of national vote at elections, and it does not seem to be able to climb out of the 5 percent range or so. However, it carries a lot of weight for its size, and for it to start making substantial noise about how Canada is not doing its part in fighting the global warming menace would certainly have a disproportionate effect on the thinking of a new center-left government just finding its feet in Ottawa.

Truth be told, such a government would probably lean in that direction in any event. The two pillars of fighting global warming in Canada would probably be the massive cutback of the environmentally dirty tar sands (excuse me while I still use the term I grew up with) and the ceasing of cutting down millions of trees from what amounts to a huge rainforest in British Columbia. These trees, of course, are supposed to absorb all sorts of greenhouse gases. The imposition of these two edicts would be economically devastating in Alberta and British Columbia.

Living in Alberta, I can make the claim (probably with a high degree of justification) that the old idea of seceding from the Canadian confederation would have a lot of supporters very quickly. Certainly this is correct if that old *Edmonton Journal* poll is still valid!

So, with a cause célèbre for going their own way, these two former Canadian provinces would probably form a nation where it would be quite clear that a large reduction in tar sands oil output (together with more traditional sources) would definitely not be high on the list of priorities for the new government.

With the forest industry in BC probably equal in importance to the oil industry in northern Alberta, it is easy to see these two erstwhile provinces pooling their resources into a new country (which I'll call ABC). The economic advantages would be large, what with a US appetite for oil, from probably any source, very high on that country's agenda. Now we may have a paradox of sorts, which I plan to discuss in a future newsletter on Hillary Clinton and her hopes and aspirations for the 2016 election.

Previously, in discussing this most ambitious woman, we have noted that in a speech to a Latino group (overflowing) in Los Angeles in November, a future President Hillary wants to bring the three NAFTA countries (Canada, the United States, and Mexico, in case you have forgotten) into a closer relationship.

As if to underline this, she is coming to Calgary, Alberta, early next month to talk about … things. It seems to me that she will be talking about oil, given the concentration of major companies in this southern Alberta city. I will read what she has to say, but I think she is having a long look at what the situation is in the United States and does not like the numbers she is seeing. In particular, she is almost certainly being told the current rubbish about the United States being self-sufficient in oil. The rationale for this belief is most likely dependent on the supply of frackable oil, which cannot last for any lengthy period of time. The supporting geology simply isn't made that way.

However, as she also undoubtedly knows, Alberta is filled with the mineral—in the tar sands. Latest figures I have seen suggest that this resource may have as much as *all* of the other conventional supplies in the world. This would amount to something like 1.6 trillion barrels of oil versus the "mere" 200 billion barrels of the Saudis.

These figures come from Wikipedia, for your information. (Yes, I know I have mentioned this in the merger chapter, but I wish to remind you of the simply staggering numbers involved.) Local scuttlebutt suggests that there is a *lot* of oil in Northern Alberta, just seems to get bigger and bigger as the technologies to extract this treasure become more and more refined. For Hillary and the US power structure in general, this is just too good to be true.

As we have been discussing in recent newsletters, if the United States is now afraid of a breakup of the various countries on the Saudi peninsula, it may be looking to redirect military forces from northeast Asia to the Persian Gulf area. (I have assessed this in the last series of newsletters on the changing situation in North Korea.)

Suddenly, almost as if the United States doesn't fully realize that Saudi Arabia is irrelevant because of Alberta, having all of the United States' oil requirements taken care of for centuries will be at the top of Hillary's agenda (as well as that of any GOP candidate who happens to win against her in 2016). The only way that all of this would make sense (i.e., going after the Middle East despite having Alberta in its backyard) would be if the United States wants it all—all the oil in the most lucrative portions of the globe, and thus denying it to anybody else. However, I think this may be better dealt with at another time in these newsletters.

Well, what happens to all of these equations if we see a new entity called ABC (maybe by the year 2018, perhaps slightly earlier is my best guess)?

What happens to the insatiable greed of US oil majors (who, interestingly enough, do not seem very interested in domestic fracking oil—a black mark on the entire subject as regards long-term availability) if Hillary's speech about NAFTA working together is suddenly thrown into confusion by global demands that Alberta stop producing the vast quantities of dirty oil?

One can only imagine, as always seems to happen in this sort of circumstance, that such an environmental demand will be put into play even as the growing global shortage becomes more acute. Obama is clearly, as far as I can see, an environmentalist, and will still not approve various Alberta/US pipelines.

Perhaps Hillary will do this, but she is also sensitive to the environment and, I believe, supports the US high priest of global warming, Al Gore. How does she manage to go after vitally needed supplies of oil for the United States and at the same time listen to an important arm of the Democratic Party: the environmental lobby? I don't know, to be honest.

Well, what happens to the new ABC, anyhow? What are its macroeconomic policies going to be? These will have to revolve around oil in Alberta and the sustainable usage of the vast forest reserves of British Columbia. I have been considering this, and it seems clear that with much of the money currently sent to Ottawa now being kept at home, ABC might do rather well.

We could look at the kingdoms in the Persian Gulf and see that the cash accruals from their oil sales are such that they can do just about anything they want. Yes, there is the growing problem of poverty in Saudi Arabia and the immense amount of youth unemployment, but the cash for the well-to-do is just about beyond limit. ABC would be better situated than the Saudis (again, taking them as an example), as there is a decent-sized manufacturing base here already—think diversification. In plain terms, there is a well-educated workforce that could be utilized as a base for expansion.

ABC will have membership in NAFTA, CETA, the EU if Harper can ever get the Europeans on side with this now long-delayed treaty, and probably the TPP (again, if Mr. Obama can ever get this away from the glare of the US right-wing blogs). There is virtually no limit to what the geographically gifted nation of ABC could accomplish.

The Alberta tax regime, which the BC portion of ABC would probably have to adopt, is very attractive as well. There are decent personal tax deductions for individuals, and the overall regime is a 10 percent flat tax. The US wealthy, not to mention their opposite numbers from heavily taxed Europe, would definitely like this. There is no lack of revenue for Alberta at present, and the provincial budget is either balanced or in a small surplus. Leaving the embrace of Ottawa would really boost the region's attractiveness in a global sense.

Enhancing the financial attractiveness of all of this separation activity would be the physical security of ABC. It would be immune from foreign invasion, and if there were anything even remotely like this threatened, the sheer power of the United States would be something that an invader would have to seriously contemplate.

Unlike Saudi Arabia, which always has to worry about Iran getting too big for its boots, or possibly Israel if relations deteriorate to the point where they were in the mid-1970s, ABC is virtually a paradise. While we cannot say that all current residents of the province would be millionaires, it is not hard to construct a scenario where housing would boom (to the great benefit of BC's immense forests) even more so than it is now. All those investing millionaires have to have a place to live, don't they?

In short, there would be a *huge* amount of investible cash available for just about any purpose whatsoever. Yes, there would be a lot of complaining from eco-groups around the world about how ABC was only interested in money and "dirty oil," but with an economic boom of immense proportions on the horizon, who would really care?

Well, what could go wrong with this overly rosy scenario? There are only two things that catch my eye immediately. Would the United States allow ABC to run its own businesses, or would it try to physically take over the new nation so that this wealth beyond imagination could be better controlled?

Would ABC be allowed to be like Saudi Arabia today, and do what it wants provided that it toes the American line, invests the huge tar sands petro-accruals in US Treasuries, and does what it is told from behind the scenes? I believe that as long as the oil flowed south through rapidly approved pipelines (e.g., Keystone), ABC would be permitted to form a new nation in the rather clogged halls of the UN.

The other scenario is more technical in nature. Currently, there seems to be a problem with getting the oil out of the tar-sand deposits because a great deal of water is required. There is only so much available. The major source of water is the Athabasca River, which empties into Lake Athabasca at Fort Chipewyan.

Despite what may be regarded as the standard denials by the oil companies, there is substantial pollution coming from the exploitation of the tar sands. I have read that for the past six thousand years, the local Indian tribes (First Nations) have lived on and made a decent living from this large body of water.

Now, for the sake of what could be powering US industry if the ABC idea becomes a reality in some sense, the locals there will simply not able to live on polluted fish and so forth, which have also called this lake their home for millennia. It is a shame, really, but it would even be more so if, in order to speed up water availability for the entire project, great dams and locks were built to bring more of this water (together with a possible changing of the flow of the Athabasca River) toward Fort McMurray to speed up what should be very profitable production.

The new federal government of ABC will have to sort out a lot of things in order to get these priceless natural resources to market in efficient quantities on an ongoing basis. It will not be easy, given the above water comments, with what should be an energy-starved world (Green and global warming concerns notwithstanding) if the backwardation in the COMEX futures pits is correct in telling us about shortages to come.

If any of my readers have any connection to the fabled Yukon Territory, I ask them to spare a few thoughts as to its future in an ABC world. There are three roads in the southern Yukon that lead out of the territory. Two of them go through Alaska, and the other is the famous Alaska Highway, which goes into British Columbia— all non-Canadian roads now! Does the Yukon join ABC, I wonder?

Well, this segment of the book deals with something I believe is definitely "on the books" and has been discussed at the highest levels of the Washington power structure. After it was agreed, with all of the relevant details, it was probably presented to the NAFTA leaders at their meeting in February 2014 in Mexico.

Can I be completely wrong with this supposition? Yes, of course I can, but I do not think so. The United States wants and needs the giant oil and water resources in Canada, and time is running short to obtain them. Reread the comments on backwardation and remember that the backwardation discounts are continuing to become somewhat larger—that is to say the shortages are becoming more pronounced. If the United States cannot take over Canada immediately, in one big chunk, then it may do so in smaller, bite-sized pieces.

In the late 1960s and early '70s, we saw maps of this in US newspapers. In 1990, a Seattle newspaper ran a similar series that showed, again, Canada being broken up into smaller units prior to United States absorption. Therefore, my comments about ABC-land are not something silly. If Washington decides that bite-sized pieces are a better way to go, then that is how it will happen. I would be remiss if I did not include this possibility in this chapter for your consideration.

With that done, if I was of a mind and had the ability to execute the merger, the first thing I would do would be to fix the exchange rate between the US and Canadian dollars in some manner. As a former foreign exchange dealer/advisor, I do know something about this. So I have reviewed all of what I have been seeing on the USD/CAD (as it known in the markets) since January 2014.

At that time, there was a lot of talk about the Canadian dollar being allowed to decline, perhaps as low as 82 US cents (or roughly 1.22 Canadian dollars per US dollar). Even the Canadian Treasury was talking about this possibility, and there was no one from higher up in the Canadian government who countered the idea. "Canadian manufacturers should be aware of this possibility" was the way it was put, or words to that effect. Major bank trading rooms advised their customers accordingly, and I must admit that I thought it made good sense for a major exporting nation such as Canada.

However, I did not know everything that was happening, and now it looks like I am wrong here (regarding a falling CAD). Right after the NAFTA gathering, we saw the Canadian dollar slam on the downward brakes, and now it has been slowly heading higher.

I would have thought that a trading band for the USD/CAD of perhaps 89 to 92 US cents might be good idea (or, 1.0870 CAD to 1.1236 USD) would give the signal that a steady exchange rate (as what happened in the EU prior to the old legacy currencies being abolished in favor of the new Euro) might be what the powers that be were looking for.

In fact, this is what happened, but the advisory desks around the world continued to tell clients (in the absence of any change from the Canadian Treasury) that the CAD was weak and would definitely see a weaker bias as the year progressed. Now, something else has happened. I think I might know what it is—*if* (big if!) the merger is going to happen.

I have mentioned that the advantage to the United States of taking over Canada might be something like US$17 trillion. This would, according to some articles I have read, have to be paid to Canadians generally along the lines of what the old East Germany (DDR) received when East and West Germany merged in 1990 (some sort of twenty-year annuity).

What I did *not* consider was what Canadians would be receiving as their end of the bargain—that is to say, in what currency they would be paid. If the USD/CAD is trading at 90 cents USD per CAD (or 1.1111 CAD per USD) on exchange day, then if Canadians are paid $17 trillion in Canadian dollars, it would only cost the US Treasury US$15.3 trillion (i.e., C$17 trillion times 0.90) or a saving of a mighty US$1.7 trillion.

This is serious money, and Canadians would probably be told "for your convenience you will be paid in CAD, to save you the worry about converting your money and the like." The average man on the street would not have any real idea of the true state of affairs!

However, what I had not properly considered was that the preference on both sides of the border throughout history have been for the two currencies to trade at par with each other. To avoid having charges laid that favoritism was being demonstrated by paying US$17 trillion to Canadians (effectively worth C$18.89 trillion or a "bonus" of C$1.89 trillion—remember these are very big numbers and will attract a *lot* of criticism if not done properly) perhaps the idea is to let the USD/CAD move back toward par.

If we do get to this target, then Canadians would be paid US$17 trillion, which would again be worth C$17 trillion. In either event, Canadians would receive the same: C$17 trillion. It would only be the paying agent, the US Treasury, which would be making the money. The receiving Canadians would be told, "We can pay you in USD or CAD. It is your choice, but as they are at par, we suggest you receive CAD—there is no difference." The two currencies at par would attract no complaints anywhere.

So what movements in the exchange rate are we seeing to justify the idea that the merger is alive and well? After vacillating between 89 and 92 US cents, the CAD has started to move somewhat higher. We are now seeing 92.5 challenged, and I am seeing comments (from the same people who were claiming that 82 cents was more likely than not) that the Canadian dollar is being sought after because "commodity currencies as a whole will do well."

I would have thought that this would imply commodities as a whole were looking to do better, but I would have been wrong. Oil is steady to lower in the last few weeks. Gold is all over the place, but the charts show that a pronounced downtrend for the yellow metal is still in play. We could fall, as my best guess, to something like sub-$1,000 before a major turnaround. This is *not* bullish action! Soft commodities (wheat, corn, and so forth) are not going higher very much if you look at them trade. So if commodities are doing nothing overtly bullish, why should commodity-based currencies (such as the CAD) be looking better and better?

Sorry, I do *not* see why, to be frank.

Therefore, if there is no reason to buy commodity currencies, there has to be something else going on. I think you can see where I am going with this. If not, it is that there is something major happening behind the scenes. The merger definitely comes to mind!

SEGMENT 3

Oil and Alternative Energy— Slippery Substance versus Slippery Politicians!

CHAPTER 1

Nukes—Are We Really Stuck
with This Monster?

Okay, so much for fun on a subject that is about as serious as one can get. Personally, I do not believe that the leaders of the industrialized world (the politicians I just referred to, in the final analysis) have any clue as to what they want to do inasmuch as a longer-term strategy is concerned. It seems all to be a "now, next year, and beyond that—who can tell?" type of arrangement.

What clueless leaders don't know, the lap-dog press (sorry to say that, but the quality of investigative journalism seems to be a lot lower than what it was when I was a boy) doesn't really care to comment about in any degree of depth. So when we talk about oil and its probable depletion, this is but one small element of the overall energy equation.

If you have been studying all about this from the press, you probably have the idea that if we can't use oil, then wind and solar are the way to go. After propounding your theories to any audience you may have, your idea has probably firmed into something resembling granite in your mind—this is what has to be done. There is no other possibility, you say, and you would be quite wrong!

I would ask you to look at nuclear power. Yes, I know that after Fukushima and what could be a horror beyond imagining evolving in the Pacific Ocean, you probably don't want to look at this possibility. Such an energy source is used all over the world, although reactors are quite expensive if all of the safety protocols are adhered to. The nuclear lobby in the United States is a strong one and, to be frank, given the very weak leadership in the US Congress, it does not look like anything substantial will happen to nuclear power to any great extent for some time.

Of course, if there is another Three Mile Island that is not caught in time, who can tell? France uses this form of electrical generation for about 70 percent of its power, and that *really* cannot be changed to any great extent without massive dislocation for the French economy.

Well, okay, you don't like nukes. To be frank, neither do I. I have always looked on nuclear power with the thought that if something goes very wrong, we might be looking at an event like Chernobyl in the modern state of Ukraine. The area around that city will be uninhabitable for possibly twenty thousand years.

If we go back in time twenty thousand years, we are looking at, in general, a caveman/mud-hut type existence. That is a long time. What happens in AD 22,000? Is man still around then to wonder about the incredible risks taken for short-term profits in a period when mankind went effectively mad? I have always looked at an analogy here, which I would like to share with you.

If you are driving in a car and have an accident, you may be injured, but you will generally be up and about at some future date to resume your life. A crash in a car need not be fatal. If you like flying and have an accident or crash, you have probably had it. You are dead, and all it took was just one accident. When it comes to nuclear power, we can say that "just one accident" can have unimaginably disastrous effects.

There is no picking up the pieces and saying that all will now be fine for us in just a few weeks or months. This is the risk with nuclear power. When it works, it works very well indeed and supplies enormous amounts of electric power for cheap domestic consumption and corporate/industrial demand.

When it goes wrong, the knock-on effects can be dangerous and life-threatening beyond measure. Is this really worth the risk? Can we match off fifty or a hundred years of problem-free generation and easy living against (in the case of Chernobyl) twenty thousand years of death and horror beyond imagination? I do not believe we can, although there are plenty of people who are willing to take the other side of this argument. As a former trader in FX and commodities, I would say that the risk/reward strategy in using nukes is simply not acceptable.

In the German newspapers in May of this year, there was a lively debate about how nuclear plants were to be disassembled in that country and how all this was going to be paid for. This is something that *really* gets my goat, and I want simply write down what I feel and why—and let my long-suffering reader judge for himself or herself.

Germany, quite rightly after the disaster ongoing at Fukushima (and probably getting much worse, but let's not go into that now), said that they were going to close down their nuclear system and decommission the nuclear power plants. Calling on the great German power companies to do this, Chancellor Merkel started to run into trouble—lots of it.

In the beginning, when Germany's government decided to get on board the nuclear power idea, they decided that they had to do this because a growing Germany was not going to be able to generate the electric power it required in any other manner. Okay, this makes sense, given what they knew about nuclear dangers at the time, but then they started to go badly wrong.

In true postwar capitalistic fashion, the government asked the German power generators to step up to the plate and find an efficient method of doing what had to be done. In an equally measured fashion, these companies simply said that the risks were too high and too expensive and that the German government would have to provide funding, and lots of it, to mitigate the risk.

This the federal German government did, and when all of the plants were built, the companies started to put the energy out to consumers, pocketing the money as profits for taking the risks they did. True, the plants were well run and there were no versions of a German Chernobyl (imagine that in a physically small country like Germany!), but private industry just soaked up the money as it came. Yes, they had to contribute to a fund which would be used to retire plants once they had reached the end of their useful lives, and today this comes to about EUR 30 billion. (It seems a lot, but read on.)

Decade in and decade out, shareholders grew fat and rich on all of this until Chancellor Merkel decided to shut them down. The companies were not happy with this at all, and in the German press in the last few days we are seeing complaints to the effect that "We can't do this ourselves. It is too expensive and the risks are too great." This was virtually the language when they set up the plants several decades ago!

What is with these big companies anyhow? They are great at cherry-picking, it seems, and are very happy to get lucrative deals for their shareholders and to tell everyone how well "the system" works. But when things go bad, they run. I suspect that they are seeing (from the benefit of being nuclear insiders) just how bad things are at Fukushima, and how hopelessly overmatched the Japanese company TEPCO is. They want no part of anything even remotely like that happening in Germany.

So this is how the western economic system works when the chips are down? This is the system that promises so much and was held up as some sort of incredible economic construct when its main competitor, the Soviet Union, failed? To set up nuclear plants took huge government support. To deconstruct them will apparently take as much or possibly even more, which will also require the German federal purse to pick up a *lot* of the financial bits and pieces. And then there is the question of nuclear waste. What have the German power companies been doing as nuclear fuel has been expended and has had to be replaced? It turns out that both the corporations and the government have done precisely nothing. The nuclear poisons are, it seems, to be someone else's problem.

"Not anymore" is what we can now write here! This will cost enormous amounts of money to resolve (if it can be resolved at all), and that is, of course, too expensive and too risky for the wretched German companies, who have unlimited access to bank credit of all types, no less.

German corporations are tucking their tails between their collective legs and sulking off a stage they should never have been on in the first place. I wonder what the Germans, running from a relatively well managed system, can tell us about the Japanese at Fukushima? There the Japanese have their concept of "face" to hide behind, but if one examines how human beings react when stressed with this subject, as is the case today, there is apparently much for the inquisitive observer (yours truly) to learn.

CHAPTER 2

Cold Fusion—Room-Temperature Nukes without the Risk?

Well, now that I have a decent fill on nuclear power, although I could go on for quite a while on that sorry subject, let me try something else. One of the things that has always interested me is cold fusion. This came out in 1989 and was discovered by Messrs. Pons and Fleishmann of the United States. What is it, anyhow?

Well, look at the sun—yep, the one in the sky. It is essentially a ball of gas with a core temperature of millions of degrees. This does all sorts of things with its atoms of hydrogen gas and effectively squeezes out a lot of energy, which heats our Earth and makes it livable. It is a complex task our sun does (we still have not yet figured it out and duplicated it well enough to generate the electric power we need), and Pons and Fleishmann wondered if it couldn't be accomplished somehow at room temperature. In other words, instead of the hot fusion that occurs on the sun, perhaps we could have cold fusion that would generate terrific amounts of energy at room temperature.

In 1989, they announced that this had been accomplished. But instead of being feted and given every Nobel Prize one can think of, they were excoriated. Almost immediately, all sorts of learned scientists (presumably those who had made their living from hot-fusion studies) were beside themselves with rage. They claimed that Pons and Fleishmann had not done enough backup research to be able to publish their works, and as such their entire idea of cold fusion was null, void, and absolutely without foundation.

I wondered about all of this. Were Pons and Fleishmann doing some sort of hush-hush (to use a word often used with "conspiracy theory" type of analysis) research to be sent to their principals for private use? While I have not seen any US comments based on this idea over the intervening twenty-five years, I do not see why it cannot be correct. If proven, it would be worth a fortune beyond measure.

Imagine, if you will, a brand-new method of fueling electricity demand throughout the globe that puts all of the older methods (including nuclear power) out of business. What a gift to mankind! What a benefit! However, cold fusion seems not to have been used to help mankind. (*Lots* of vested interests here, I would imagine, who would like nothing better than to keep the decaying status quo operational for as long as possible.)

However, not all research is done in the United States, as there are many other countries with very pressing power needs. Let us consider Japan. This small island nation (less than half the size of Alberta, but with a population of more than thirty times greater) has few natural resources. They have to import all of their petroleum needs, and for them nuclear power (or anything else, come to think of it) is of critical importance. So if they see something like cold fusion, they are going to jump all over it. This they did, and set up all sorts of research labs to see if they could use what Pons and Fleishmann had apparently discovered. I followed this for several years and saw all sorts of results.

Some Japanese labs duplicated the results of the Americans, and others had no luck whatsoever. Still others had mixed results that they were unable to reproduce at all. The Russians were interested, but the net effect is that there does not seem to be a consensus on what Pons and Fleishmann were able to accomplish. What troubles me is that all of the nearly frenzied lab work done on their experiments suddenly came to a halt shortly after the turn of the century, and nothing further has been announced.

There are two possibilities here. Either there is nothing left to research and Pons and Fleishmann have been proven to be frauds, or else this *has* been proven to work and is being held off the markets for reasons of the immense profit potential. (Politicians being slippery here?)

I think, after reviewing all of the material I can find on cold fusion, that it is a valid possibility. If it *is* being held back because of profit concerns and so forth, then mankind deserves just about everything that is probably going to happen to us—probably in not that long a period of time.

However, while we should file cold fusion away for future reference, as it will almost certainly be brought to the surface again, there are other things to be trotted out. I would now like to examine what is called, somewhat grandly, solar power. This is, not surprisingly, energy derived from the sun, which is not likely to go out for a *very* long time (several billion years, at current estimates). This sounds almost too good to be true, doesn't it?

CHAPTER 3

Solar Power: Something We Can All Understand? Nope!

The understanding I referred to at the end of the last chapter may not be the case. I watched, for many years, a huge EU project in the Sahara Desert in Africa. The project was designed to get this most inhospitable piece of land to bloom "with a thousand points of light"—well, sort of. You probably know this expression of former President George Bush, but it should probably interpreted to get the Sahara to bloom "with a thousand solar collectors."

With all of the sunlight that falls on this massive desert, this sort of solar power generator should have been a no-brainer. Nope! You got that one wrong. Have a look at what I wrote in my newsletter not that long ago about this:

> Do you remember the great initiative by the EU some years back called DESERTEC? It was an attempt to effectively set up a series of solar

collectors from across the Sahara and transfer the resulting energy back to the European power grids through Italy. It was an immense project, but the then Green EU decided that it was all worth it, and they trumpeted the immense benefits every chance they got.

Politicians lined up to be interviewed, and the costs, we were assured, were not that serious when one considered the never-ending supply of electricity that would be generated. After all, when does the Sahara Desert become cloudy? Plans went ahead with the usual gusto until, one day, it all stopped. Politicians were suddenly "too busy" to answer questions about all of this, and interest waned with an almost indecent haste.

The idea put out was that with all of the potential civil wars in North Africa, the whole project was just too risky. That was all that was said, if I remember correctly, although there was some talk that technologically speaking the project wouldn't work, and the matter dropped out of sight.

A mess, to be sure, but the math, despite all of the official blather from greasy and slippery politicians, simply didn't work. It then turned out that the science was not really all that good, either. To generate solar power, there has to be certain return for shareholders—assuming we stick with the wretched system where the free market tells us what wonderful things can be done but doesn't really deliver all that often.

We also have to be aware that to deliver the end product to market means that it has to be cheaper than other effective sources. This would include the wretched nuclear power, which has never been what was promised in the beginning of its heyday.

Oil has been plentiful for more than a century now (we, in Alberta, are celebrating the first oil wells drilled here a hundred years ago this year), and it has been something that will "always be there" even though it is patently clear that this can never be. Oil is cheap relative to many other possible energy sources, and certainly when compared to solar power. Therefore, why make the sun work for its keep when we can just use oil?

Yes, it is true that in the beginning a new technology will frequently cost a great deal more, but that is before all sorts of new refinements are found and developed that will make the new technology cheaper. What happens when it is revealed that solar power does not and *cannot* work?

In what has to have been a really terrific slap in the face to proponents of this form of "renewable energy," the EU (as can be seen from my newsletter clipping above) simply decided that it didn't work and couldn't work. One day, the EU's brain trust (a term I use very loosely) decided to recheck the figures from the energy nirvana that was supposed to be DESERTEC.

They found, to their horror, that the electricity being claimed from the Sahara would barely light a series of homes and lighthouses in Sicily—just across a narrow portion of the Mediterranean Sea from Africa! It seems that the technical skills required to send all this power north to the EU's industrial powerhouse, Germany, simply wasn't there. It had been assumed that this would exist, and that seemed to be a rather poor assumption.

I follow a US equity called First Solar, or FSLR, which is what it trades under on the NASDAQ. For several years after its inception, it traded very nicely under the assumption that solar power was here to stay and was the wave of the future. The euphoria that the transition from an oil-based economy was not based on the reality of the nuts-and-bolts world simply was not seriously considered. The free market, with all of its mysterious and little-understood theories of market efficiencies, was simply assumed to be able to provide whatever solutions were required.

When it became clear (assisted by the rumored bankruptcy of a low-cost solar panel maker in China) that the entire idea of solar power was simply a chimera, the stock crashed from something like $170 to about $10. This is quite a fall! As I write these words in the spring of 2014, it has recovered to about $70 or so, which is a decent enough bounce, but is it anything more than this?

After all, if a low-cost producer in China cannot make the producers cheap enough for solar panels for western economies and the technology is suspect at best, what is the purpose of solar power even existing, much less FSLR and its competitors? I addressed this in my newsletters over the DESERTEC commentary above.

What follows is also a decent commentary on what is probably official EU thinking as well. I think that what I wrote then is quite good enough for now, and I shall prove this (hopefully to your satisfaction) to a greater extent in the forthcoming paragraphs. Here is another brief newsletter clipping:

> The United States and the EU have lots of money and credit to take a major flyer on something like DESERTEC, if either so chose. The money, through official channels in one form or another, is simply not forthcoming now. I wonder whether the stock market got wind of this, and this is the reason why First Solar was driven through the floor two years ago.
>
> If the money (as with wind power) is not available for something that is so critical for the EU, then something is seriously wrong somewhere, to be admitted or not. The EU, to come full circle with this set of essays, knows a very great deal about what is happening with various forms of power generation and has decided, being nice and quiet in true bureaucratic fashion, that there is very little alternative (if any) to simple, good old-fashioned oil.
>
> This is true in a traditional sense from experience over the last century or so, and so we go down the fracking trail, which, if many US oil engineers are to be listened to, is only a temporary palliative at best. What is the EU going to do, now that they have effectively said that they are bankrupt of new ideas and can only feebly embrace technologies they have scorned quite openly—at least until a few months ago?

Needless to say, this is all very bad news for Europe.

Okay, so what did the EU do then? Well, it seems to have taken a page out of the modern US book for oil drilling and has endorsed fracking. The EU is supposedly one of the greenest entities on the face of the planet, and fracking (usually considered dirty oil) is what the Germans might refer to as *verboten!* Here is an interesting essay from the leading German newspaper *der Spiegel* on this (emphasis mine):

> Europe may be backing away from its ambitious climate protection goals.
>
> *The EU's reputation as a model of environmental responsibility may soon be history. The European Commission wants to forgo ambitious climate protection goals and pave the way for fracking—jeopardizing Germany's touted energy revolution in the process.*[4]

Well, when the EU comes full circle on this, they *really* don't play around! Interestingly enough, I didn't see any follow on articles about this in the German press (which I personally regard as among the most environmentally conscientious in the EU). It also says a great deal. Oil is going to be in our future for a long time to come, no matter

---

4   Gregor Peter Schmitz, "Green Fade-out: Europe to Ditch Climate Protection Goals," *der Spiegel,* January 15, 2014, http://www.spiegel. de/international/europe/european-commission-move-away-from-climate-protection-goals-a-943664.html.

how the art of fracking manages to hold up—it is a short-run phenomenon at best. The "best minds" in the EU have come to this conclusion, and that is apparently that.

So the EU has effectively thrown in the towel on climate change, and given the level of brainpower in Brussels, I suspect that there may be something else in play. I shall return to this a bit later on, but before we leave my commentary on solar power, I should look at what the UN has been saying about this.

One would have thought that on such an important subject as essentially saving the world from manmade climate changes (if this is, as Al Gore suggests, correct), people from around our planet would be talking to each other on an ongoing basis. This does not seem to be so. As has been the case with so many major possibilities in history, the world is divided into major power blocs, each with its own agenda for dominating a particular theme.

How is this so? Well, we have just had a good look at how the European power bloc (as represented by the EU) feels about fracking, and how they have changed their minds completely on what this represents to the future of Europe. What about the UN?

To be frank, I have never been a fan of the United Nations. It is a cesspit of political intrigue that daily disproves its founding principles of mankind working together. I remember well in the Reagan Administration when, at a press conference, someone pointed out that the UN had condemned something the administration had done. In any event, it incurred the wrath of the White House, and in a press conference the speaker basically told the reporter who had brought up the question, "Who cares what a debating society two hundred miles from here thinks?" The speaker was never disciplined for these supposedly intemperate remarks, which can only lead one to assume that he spoke as he did with the full backing of the powers that be in Washington.

Today, whenever Washington wants something done, it is always "the will of the international community" when it is approved. When something is *not* done, it is "such-and-such country has once again flouted the will of the international community"—as if there is any such thing in reality.

So given that the major world powers apparently feel little more than contempt for the UN and what it apparently stands for, is it any wonder that little in the way of communication is accomplished between New York and, say, the EU? Again, in my view, the sooner this joke of a debating society is wound up, the better off we shall be.

Okay, now that I have got that off my chest, I can make the simple comment that it's no wonder the UN comes out with a long-term energy plan that apparently runs completely counter to what the EU has had to say in at least a portion of its report. British newspaper the *Telegraph* came out with a very good story not that long ago about how we are all going to have to adopt renewables as our main source of energy in the balance of this century. Have a look: "Governments must switch from fossil fuels to nuclear, wind, and solar energy to avoid a global-warming catastrophe in a move costing about £300 billion a year, a United Nations report warns."[5]

---

5   Robert Mendick, "UN Green Police Say Ditch Oil and Change Your Diet," *The Telegraph,* April 12, 2014, http://www.telegraph.co.uk/earth/environment/climatechange/10763080/UN-green-police-say-ditch-oil-and-change-your-diet.html.

In reviewing this brief story, I am struck by the concept that the "big brains" at the various UN agencies—this outfit just grows and grows bureaucratically, with *you* paying for it—have come to the conclusion that we have to decarbonize the world and adopt renewables. We are also seeing something I do not like, and that is the fact that we shall all have to change our diets.

This means, in all probability, that we westerners are going to have to get along with less red meat, as there may be less grain to feed the cattle that much of our diet come from. This belief seems rooted in the consciousness of UN planners, despite the fact that cattle are much tastier when reared on grass. Just turn them loose on the open prairie and you will have better cattle with better meat—with the obvious corollary that there will be a lot of grain freed up for other more pressing needs.

However, grain and some sort of growing political belief that it is somehow "wrong" to eat poor, defenseless cattle is going to become a growing UN-inspired problem as we move forward.

Let us return to the decarbonized world. I have studied this for many years—decades—and I simply cannot agree with what they are saying. The basic idea of the UN think tanks is that the atmosphere of the world is being heavily polluted by the mass burning and consumption of hydrocarbons, and this will have to be radically curtailed.

Many US right-wingers feel that what the UN would really like to do is to push mankind (read: Americans) into larger and larger cities with very limited mobility. The idea is that with a large chunk of Americans in such living conditions, most of the rest will be left on existing farms to provide food for the cities and to grow that food under very strict protocols. The rest of the country would be given back to nature, to allow Mother Earth to heal herself from the raping it has endured under man's tutelage for so many centuries now.

What strikes me is that this Agenda 21 (as it has come to be called after its presentation in Rio de Janerio in 1992) is assumed to be the only solution for what are admittedly very real problems on the face of an increasingly exhausted planet. All of this planning is quite remarkable for what is little more than a global debating society! There are, of course, many other solutions to what we have to face up to in the coming decades, and we shall examine these as this book progresses.

As I was saying above, the UN seems to regard itself as some sort of unerring institution, and its dictates are to be obeyed because they are the product of the "very finest minds" the planet has to offer. I am sure that the EU would not agree with this at all. The big thing to note here is that EU thinkers tend to regard what has to be done from a more practical bent.

They were all quite happy with the concept of solar power until they were apparently convinced that their desires (planned society?) were not achievable. They changed, as we have discovered, to adopting the idea of frackable oil and natural gas—possibly inspired by a potential Russian boycott of the EU if things got nasty with the Ukraine, which they clearly have. How long will they continue with this unusual (for them) tactic?

With the EU's economy close to ruins, as the EU is starting to find out that not all countries can use a currency (the Euro) that is suitable for Germany and few others, they cannot afford further declines. However, this means little to the UN, it seems. There we have a mandate, as the *Telegraph* article strongly implies, that renewables will be the way to go. Oblivious to the fact that the science may not work at all, the implied comment from the UN is that we have to make it work. This is an audacious and, frankly, arrogant approach for the debating society to adopt for the world.

Well, let us finish off the comments on solar power by returning to our friend FSLR. We have noted that its price soared into the financial stratosphere when it started operations on wild optimism that solar power would be a large portion of what was needed to save mankind from being cooked to death by global warming, as well as fueling our insane desire to burn as much fossil fuel as possible for generally minor things—such as long-distance driving on vacations and the like.

We could also note here that another so-called frivolous item would be the practice of growing iceberg lettuce in California and trucking it three thousand miles to markets in Maine. However, that is an Agenda 21 worry—not ours—so let us return to what FSLR's stock price might be telling us.

We have seen that it went from an absurd overvaluation in the $160–$170 range all the way down to $10 or so briefly. Then what happened? As is usual with this sort of price collapse, there were the generally dismal stories that FSLR didn't have the cash to keep going and that it would not be able to sell solar panels because of severe price undercutting from China.

Then the Chinese firm went bankrupt because "it couldn't make a go of solar," and on and on it went. These things are typical of a market bottom where any and all rumors, no matter how wild, are deemed to be newsworthy. However, someone did start buying down there (an insider who couldn't believe the bargain FSLR represented, perhaps—it happens), and we started to rebound slowly.

In May 2014, it looks quite good at near $70. If you are a technical analysis person, or at least sympathetic to the concept, we can say that it has now retraced all of the losses to this level, which happens to be the two-hundred-week simple moving average.

Technical theory now holds that if we can break this to the upside on a weekly close and then open higher the next week, we probably have a good intermediate term buying signal. Of interest, we did try for week after week some months ago to break through this major moving average, and it looks like we have failed because the market has come back lower, to the $58 area. (This is before it bounced back to close through the $70 barrier.)

By the way, while I have your attention, please do not say something like, "Moving averages? They are just wiggly lines on a bit of paper which mean nothing at all." I took my first lesson in "wiggly lines" back in 1962 when this science was popular, in general, in certain areas of the dealing community. They are *still* popular, and if they had no significance, this would not be the case among cash-starved and profit-hungry dealers.

Anyway, to finish off my story on FSLR, let me say that we can still break the $70 line, although perhaps not immediately, and when that happens we shall see buyers of all descriptions pile in to buy "because the technical signal has been broken and if I don't buy someone else will." True enough, I guess, but what does this say about buying a security on the basis of "the fundamentals are good and are likely to be so for a long time to come"?

In other words, it doesn't matter if solar power is a viable idea or not. People will buy because others are buying (again, so much for independent thought and analysis) and the rumor will be "the insiders are buying, and if it is good enough for them, then it is good enough for me!" To put all of this yet another way, this stock can go to the moon because it is the "wave of the future."

It makes no difference if the future leaves this technology in the dust; its stocks will be bought anyhow. Read the bit about the UN I wrote earlier on. The UN says that it must work, and accordingly it will be made to work. (Hey, if it is good enough for the world's premier debating society …)

Well, let's bring an end to this chapter on solar power, at least for now. It seems clear to me that with so many really well-to-do types who apparently believe in solar power, something will be found to support this concept and bring it to the attention of the ever-gullible public.

Any losses, as so often happens, will probably be lumped onto these poor souls via the mechanism of a collapsing share price. The profits, assuming that the technical difficulties can be overcome and some sort of viable system comes to the fore to rescue the debating society, will go to where profits usually go, I suspect (enough said). Just remember the lessons of DESERTEC. If a power-starved society like the EU cannot make a go of solar power in an area of the world which is about as solar-friendly as it is possible to get (the Sahara Desert), it is going to take a *great* breakthrough to make all of this finally work at all.

CHAPTER 4

Wind Power—Yet Another Bag of Hot Air? (Guess What I Am Going to Say Here!)

And now let me pass along to another great hope for the future of our energy hungry society, and that is wind power. Yes, when someone first mooted this as a possible solution to the energy crisis, we all heard comebacks of "hot air" or some such. However, the powers that be (great debaters one and all—sorry, I really do have a bee in my bonnet about the UN, don't I?) said otherwise.

We were then all treated to visions of old-fashioned Dutch windmills from centuries past and told that a modern version of this would use all of the free energy from moving air. In turn, this would power small generators in the windmills to churn out all of the electricity that a modern society could ever want or need.

We were all told that the free market would find the solutions we all needed and life would go on as before. All we needed was the right incentive and lots of government money in the form of grants and the like. In other words, we should throw money at the problem willy-nilly and simply hope that some of it sticks.

Now, as you may have gathered by now, I am a big believer in government intervention for the simple reason that governments never have to worry what shareholders think: when something has to be done that is very expensive, a proper intervention policy would save uncounted amounts of money.

I am going to wander off subject to make a point, which I hope will come back to illustrate what we have found to be the fallacies of wind power. You read that correctly—this doesn't work either, but that will not stop the Great Debaters from simply declaring that this is what we have to look forward to and that it will work!

Anyhow, for the point at issue immediately, let me revert back to nuclear power and what Germany is doing to phase out this ghastly electricity-generating medium.

I refer you to one simple thing that was used in the United States to sell nuclear energy to an ever-gullible American public (sorry if you take offense at these words—it is just a fact of life, at least with nuclear power).

We were told, and I remember this from when I was much younger, that nuclear power would make electricity "too cheap to even monitor." I don't know about you, but I am still waiting for my first electric bill reading "Amount Due: $0.00." The sheer absurdity of this statement makes one wonder.

Why would any company even consider getting involved with such a method of generating electricity when the returns, by definition, must be zero? Why didn't people and slippery politicians even think to ask such simple questions? Now the questions are *much* more difficult and are probably beyond response. We now see much more difficult questions arising amidst the obvious shortcomings over wind power.

So to return to wind power and its initially great expectations, we should be able to look at the EU for a good guide as to where this area of experimentation is going. After the Falkland Islands, with an average wind speed of about twenty miles per hour all day, the windiest pace on the planet is located at Horns Rev, Denmark (a member of the EU). With the constant flow of wind from the sea, it was thought to be a no-brainer for Denmark to be a leader in wind power technology.

It turns out that the powers that be did not fully understand what was happening when they jumped all over this particular bandwagon, thinking that it was a sure thing (as if there is ever such an animal). Well, as is with the case with solar power, it turns out that wind power is also less than functional. In other words, it really doesn't work either from a monetary perspective or from a mechanical/theoretical analysis. Sigh. Some things never change, do they?

With EU governments pouring money into wind power and great columns of windmills being constructed across the North Sea, the feeling was that wind power would prove its worth. Great subsidies were also paid out to landowners who leased large tracts of their properties to up-and-coming companies that were anxious to prove what they could do in this new modern age.

I wondered at the time (using the British model because Britain has a great number of gales from autumn and winter storms) how such huge subsidies could be factored into the final price structure for the end product of these windmills. It can't, at least not if it wishes to be competitive with other power sources (including solar power). Nevertheless, the EU plodded on with their plans.

Finally, the German press stood up and told the world that the Horns Rev. project was a colossal waste of money and could not possibly work. If we follow the money, always a good path in assessing a new technology, we see (as noted previously) that the EU wishes to go back to fracking: about as unrenewable a source of energy as one can get.

In setting up the windmills in the North Sea, the planners did not seem to have factored into their calculations the corrosive effects of saltwater on windmills, which may stand idle for some periods of time when the wind does not blow as projected. (Which grade school did they get their engineers from? I must somewhat acerbically ask.)

They also found that winds blow mainly at night in that area of the world and, surprise, surprise, most people in Denmark and neighboring areas of Germany are asleep at that time and use very little of the power being generated. Then they found out that when electricity *was* being generated, there was no good way to store it for when it would be required by the consumers. In other words, Denmark might be able to generate all sorts of power from the North Sea, but it was effectively useless!

The German would-be consumers were angry and had to turn to other sources for their electricity (nuclear power raises its ugly head here). They billed, under contract, the Danes for the difference between their nonexistent power and traditional nuclear energy. So from a sure thing, where there would be pots of money for all concerned (see my comments on nuclear power), the Danes actually found a way to lose on the deal! Amazing. As far as I know, these problems have not yet been resolved.

The only place where windmills have worked has been in the Falkland Islands, where power can be generated twenty-fours a day because of the wind flow down there. As an aside here, one must compliment the planning department of the Falklands government in Port Stanley. Someone there noticed that as a British Crown Colony, it is considered part of Great Britain. This being the case, the Falklands should be eligible for a generous subsidy from Brussels! Anyhow, on the basis of "nothing ventured, nothing gained," they applied for this subsidy on these grounds and got it.

So the EU is subsidizing a place that is about as far away from the EU as one can get. The farmers who use this facility to supplement their electricity generation on the very remote farms down there are doing very well, I understand, versus the huge diesel costs which they had to pay previously with inefficient generators. Well, I'm glad this works in at least one area of the EU, anyway. Too bad it cannot be used elsewhere in the EU because the wind, as noted, is simply generated at the wrong time for the customers who need it. (Solution: move the EU to the Falklands?)

Another problem noted with windmills (British windmills in this case) was that there was too much wind. These windmills have a safety factor that shut them down when wind speeds exceed a certain limit—I believe this is a hundred miles per hour. In some of the really severe gales, this has been exceeded and has resulted in jammed motors, locked windmill blades, and fires on occasion when the motors simply could not handle the stress.

I also saw, in the British press, pictures of windmills being knocked down by sheer pressure of airflow from storms. It seems to me that windmills lying on the ground in flames are not going to generate that much in the way of electricity. British landowners also found out, in their crazed greed for easy money from the government, that the sheer noise from blades turning at high speeds can ruin a decent night's sleep and make living anywhere near these wretched devices very difficult indeed. Another problem was that windmills and migratory birds simply do not mix well—unless you like seeing bits of birds that look like they have been strained through a giant sieve.

The EU and the UK are not the only places with windmill problems. I am fortunate enough to receive updates, issued from time to time, by the legendary oilman T. Boone Pickens of the United States. Now in his eighties, he is still looking for new technologies and ways to make money from them.

It seems to me that he also has what is quite rare for any entrepreneur these days: a love of his country and the desire to do what is right to keep it on top, which means solving its growing energy difficulties. For quite some time, he has been championing the cause of wind power as an answer to a major part of America's energy woes.

In a letter to his "army," he trumpeted America's staggering wind potential as he saw it and boldly proclaimed that wind coming off the Pacific Ocean into the Pacific Northwest (and California, one presumes) would make the United States the "Saudi Arabia of wind power." I am not sure what the Falkland Islands would say about this; ditto Horns Rev. and Alberta's own Pincher Creek, the third-windiest place on the planet.

Pickens did what he considered his due diligence and got to the point where he told his "army" one day that he was going to meet some very influential people in Washington, DC, about what he wanted to do to start his plans of operation. He was optimistic and thought that he would get some sort of subsidy to back up his claims and plans. Given that this is how things get done in the United States and given how many advanced nations elsewhere in the world have handled this approach, I suppose he was not being unrealistic. Well, he went to Washington, saw his people and … came home with precisely zero in funding or grants!

He said nothing about what happened, or rather didn't happen, but as this was taking place at about the time that the EU was seeing problems with wind power, I think he was told that he had better forget the whole thing because it didn't work, financially or technically.

It must have been a bitter blow, given the effort he put into what he believed was correct. I do not believe that the oil companies gave Washington a strong financial incentive to shoot him down. It is what it is, and Pickens simply struck out. Now he talks about oil and the various ways that this can be better used to make America energy-independent. I can't see this, given the very limited life span of fracking, but that is what he is talking about: energy from whatever petroleum-based source can be found and accessed.

In considering this dismal subject (wind power, that is), I should look at the Danish company Vestas, traded on the pink sheets in New York under the symbol VWSYF. In many respects, this is like what we saw with the US company FSLR. It started out life as if people could not get enough of what was on offer—so great was the belief that this, indeed, was time to get involved with alternative energy and wind power. The stock soared to DKK 690 or so in 2009 ($1.00 = DKK 5.50, Denmark being one of the few countries in the EU to still use its own currency and not the Euro).

Then we started to see stories about technical problems with windmills and the unique (but nonetheless valid) worries about offshore-sited windmills. The price of the stock crashed, and at its low point it traded at something like $4/DKK 22—quite a drop from DKK 690. Worries about the financial stability of the company surfaced, despite the vast sums available to it from the Danish and EU governments, and the CEO was forced out. Now, did what happened with FSLR happen with Vestas? Did it bounce off the bottom?

Yes, it did. Currently it is trading at about DKK 270–280, with the trading patterns on the charts looking very bullish indeed. Personally, I would not chase after this stock if I wanted to buy it but instead would wait for some sort of pullback and then scale in purchases. Your mileage may vary.

So given that it has traded in a very similar pattern to FSLR, what can we say about the underlying fundamentals? Regrettably, people are once again buying because "if we don't, everyone else will buy." So when everyone else staggers off the edge of the cliff, you are going to do so as well? Apparently, this is the case.

The debating society extraordinaire in New York has again decreed (well, effectively so, anyway) that wind power must be made to work, and so, because the "great thinkers" have decreed this, the lemmings rush to buy Vestas as fast as they can because it must obviously be a money spinner! These same people might hate the concept of the UN with a passion, but when an alternative energy decree comes out of those intellectually clogged corridors, they rush to buy. They are caught in the idea of "Let's make money any way we can, whether we understand it or not!"

CHAPTER 5

Hydroelectricity—Yes, This Is a Decent Renewable (They Finally Found One That Works)

So solar power and wind power either do not work or else need a lot of further research, to be kind about it. What other sources do our intellectual betters have in mind? There have been all sorts of wondrous ideas trotted out, but what do they really do in the final analysis (with one possible exception, which looks like being torpedoed by political concerns)?

We have biomass, tidal power, natural gas (now a favorite of Mr. Pickens), geothermal power, and hydroelectric power. The latter has been around for many years now and comprises a lot of electricity for power-hungry North America (read: the United States, in particular the northeast). However, to deal with hydro first, there are problems brewing, and these tie in directly with the merger we mentioned earlier on in the book.

Hydroelectricity is formed, basically, when man dams a large, fast-flowing river and uses the action of the water to spin turbines, which in turn generate a lot of electricity. The giant rivers of northern Quebec and in Labrador (part of the Canadian province of Newfoundland, for those who may have doubts) send vast amounts of this precious resource via giant power pylons (and these really are huge—I have seen them) to the US markets. There are two difficulties to be overcome here, and I do not believe that either has been really addressed.

First is that these giant dams have an average lifespan of about fifty years. I remember in the mid-1970s, both Quebec and Labrador were caught up in the midst of a terrific building boom. I worked in the bank branch that did all of the financial transfers for the major Labrador projects, and they were massive. We are now not far from the fifty-year timeline, and I have seen precious little which tells me that either the Newfoundland or Quebec governments have set aside cash reserves to repair and restore these dams or even try to build new projects.

It seems that both governments are simply content to rake in the hydro cash, in one form or another, and spend it as fast as possible. They have fallen into the easy trap of thinking that these flows of funds will continue as long as the water flows continue to spin the turbines, and that will be (of course) forever. The hydro dividends are now a structural part of spending programs for these two governments, and it could be very difficult to disengage from such receipts and actually spend money rectifying any potential problems for the existing dam structure.

Well, something will have to be done. We can also say that the current series of dams tend to accumulate naturally occurring dirt from river flows (silt), which will, over time, clog intake pipes and so forth. This will, at the very least, reduce the output of critically needed hydropower. It may be that the relevant hydro corporations spend time and money removing the silt, but it is not something one hears about.

One also does not hear, apart from very irritated Indian tribes (or Native Americans if you prefer), that the flow of fish is also reduced. Many of these local tribes need to live on fish, as have their ancestors for thousands of years. It is probable, sorry to say, that this lifestyle is to be freely sacrificed so that the unending demand for hydropower can continue to be supplied without significant interruption to the industrial estates in the northeastern United States.

I feel fairly confident in writing this, as in my home province of Alberta there is much controversy about the toxic runoff from the tar sands reaching Lake Athabasca and causing severe distress to the Indian and First Nations communities around the remote town of Fort Chipewyan in northern Alberta.

What I suspect will happen is twofold. In the 1970s, the imaginative Premier of Quebec Robert Bourassa (nicknamed Bob le Job for his unusual means of hydro development, which would promote Quebec employment) was actually considering building a hundred-mile dam across the mouth of James Bay, which lies at the bottom end of Hudson Bay.

The idea was that the massive flow of water between the two bays would generate unimaginable amounts of hydropower, most probably for export to the United States. The financing would have been daunting, estimated at something like $100 billion, which would have been a formidable amount to raise in the post-1974 financially scarred landscape. The technical problems where also cited as being "insurmountable," which is politician-speak for "don't even try this and risk humiliating me." The plan went nowhere, needless to say.

What I want to mention now is the second of the two points noted above. What happens to all this if the merger between Canada and the United States goes ahead? The United States has unlimited amounts of the world's reserve currency and can finance anything it wants on this continent. If the technology was not available in 1975 or so (i.e., the James/Hudson Bay project), is it available today?

With the enormous advances in computer science and engineering since then, I am willing to bet that it is. Certainly, the geographical imperatives surrounding the US economy these days (the acute demand for water, if nothing else) would make some sort of effort mandatory on the part of the newly merged governments of Canada and the United States.

Economic growth, the mantra of US industry, would demand new and more powerful energy sources. Besides damming the great rivers of northern Canada for more hydropower, the James/Hudson Bay project would be irresistibly attractive. It is quite possible, in my opinion, that the prime movers and shakers who really run the US economy might have had this project (among others) in mind when they started their merger project. Time will tell, but economic imperatives cannot be ignored on this scale.

CHAPTER 6

Biomass—Let's Burn Our Way to Energy Independence

So there is a lot of interest in northern Canada, as far as I can see. This and the Alberta tar sands will keep merger talks alive and well, of that I am sure. However, while a merger within North America would satisfy a lot of queries about how we will manage, there must be other possibilities. Solar and wind power I am justifiably skeptical on, so what do we look at next?

There are other minor options right now, such as biomass. This is a fancy way of saying "burning wood chips, logs, and basically anything that grows and is combustible." The sellers of this idea tell us of the wonderful ways that we can use it. We can thin out forests that are clogged with all sorts of undergrowth and very prone to fires. If one looks at the wildfires that very often burn out of control in dry states such as California, we see that they start and expand rapidly because of excessive undergrowth.

In assessing this further, we see many ecologists who do not want to see Mother Nature "hurt" in some manner (such hurting being critical to Mother Nature's managing vast areas of forests). It must be clear, therefore, that they have little idea what they are protecting. The undergrowth has to be cleared, and if man will not allow this to happen, then there are more extreme ways—wildfires—of getting it done.

What irritates me about this method of providing energy through controlled burns, which can heat water and turn turbines and the like, is that what one group of ecologists want to happen is often bitterly opposed by others. Speaking personally, I have never understood biomass and its appeal. Surely we can run out of forests long before the real energy shortages have been addressed, and I am allowing for the "managed forest" theory, which holds that we can plant forests and nurture them to grow and expand to meet production quotas and goals.

Sorry, but nature doesn't work like that! Go and find a forest somewhere and walk in it, and then have a good look-see at how nature has put it together. Nature puts different kinds of trees all in the same general area and with different spacing and so forth. In today's planned forest, we see the same kind of tree (the kind which brings the maximum profit to a logging company) planted a few feet apart in perfect rows.

So what, you may ask? Simply this: What happens if disease breaks out in the trees planted by man through his forest companies? The trees are not separated by other types of trees, so the disease or insect infestation will roar through the single-growth forest at an incredible rate. The infected trees will then be good for little, if anything. If there are a dozen different types of trees in a natural forest, then it is a fair bet that the disease may not spread as fast or at all.

If we do get a disease in a real forest, it may even be slow enough to be treated by the forest company concerned. We can also wonder about forest creatures. A forest is composed of trees of all sorts, as well as an amazing number of different animals, all of which interact with the trees and plants that grow there. In leveling a forest to provide for biomass energy, one will destroy or severely restrict the life habitats of these animals.

There are plenty of eco-groups that would be appalled by this sort of thing. In other words, boiling all of this down to its basics, we can say that biomass, apart from a few special cases, really isn't going to be anything of consequence.

Another version of the biomass concept would be geothermal energy, which, as its name implies, is a way of using what Americans might refer to as a hot spring. The ground, principally as the result of a volcanic or hot area, gives forth hot water, steam, or other allied products. This is energy and can be used as such, and its proponents talk about this being an endless cycle of "free energy" because rainfall will replenish the hot water that is taken out.

This sounds fine, but again it fails in practice. California looked at this, I am told, in the late 1980s and found that the rainwater did not fall fast enough to replenish what was taken out for energy purposes. Given that California may be at the start of a five-hundred-year drought, as some climatologists have claimed, this shortage of rainfall is not going to do the idea of geothermal energy much good at all. Forget it, again, except in areas where there might be a better balance between hot water and rainfall.

CHAPTER 7

Okay, Is There Anything You Like That May Actually Work? (Well, Yes, Now That You Mention It!)

In this segment of the book, I have been discarding some of the more widely held ideas hand over fist. These are wind power, solar power, biomass, geothermal, and of course my favorite *bête-noir*, nuclear energy. So what is left? Well, there are two things I personally like and which the politicians are apparently not that happy with.

These are not well known outside of the ink-splashed ideas just mentioned, but seem to be efficient for microscale generators. Is micro the way to go, and not the huge and inefficient ideas routinely trumpeted about? The above ideas are examples of the outworn "bigger is better" concept.

One "micro" idea is the Bedini Schoolgirl motor, which I wish to write a little bit on and which has been derided as a perpetual motion machine by scientists. These words are merely a nasty way of saying, "This device can never work—stop wasting your time on it." Hmmm … sounds like the reception given to cold fusion, doesn't it?

The other possibility hasn't even been discussed at the Bedini level, but it sounds like something of the common sense variety. The theory is that mankind is killing itself by pumping huge amounts of carbon dioxide, carbon monoxide, and carbon anything-else-you-can-think-of into the air. Gasoline engines have been excoriated by all of this, but why? The technology may well exist to take out of the atmosphere the stuff we put into it and to simply use it again. Presto! Atmosphere cleaned, and energy demand met to a decent extent.

Sadly, I do not think we shall see either of these possibilities put into play. I have referred to the derision heaped on the Bedini Schoolgirl motor. The "schoolgirl" portion of this refers to a schoolgirl in the United States who had a science project to do for school (doesn't it always seem to be like this?) and was running late. Either, depending on whom you read, she got her inspiration from her father and his interest in magnets or saw something that triggered something in her mind to try something with magnets.

She received a very high grade for her efforts, and I read that when her motor was started up, it was still running five days later. The trouble here is that this sort of thing did not get picked up by a major company and patented (which would effectively remove it from circulation as a serious consideration) because it is very simple to put together and use.

The big thing here is that this device can be used on a micro level instead of the usual macro level one usually associates with major breakthroughs. Make no mistake about it: it *is* significant. It can be used, if there were a disaster affecting the economic dissemination of electric power, by individual homes quite easily.

If one is conspiracy-minded, one could say that the powers that be do not want this technology to be widely known (sort of like cold fusion, it occurs to me), as there is no profit in it for captive corporations. If there is a major power outage for any reason (EMP attacks have been mooted once again in recent months), these controlling interests want people helpless and not "managing to get by" on a very small scale.

In any event, it is my opinion that if any of my readers want to investigate, they could do a lot worse than the Bedini Schoolgirl motor. I have seen it used in various formats on farms in Australia's remote outback with good success. The Falklands, if they were not so blessed with their abundant wind power, would find this device very useful as well.

And what can we say about the second of our two "unknown" technologies, that of reclaiming carbon from the atmosphere? This sounds rather obvious, but it also lies in the area where the militant environmentalists have staked their claims to fame. How often have you looked at news stories about the terrible damage to the ozone layer (and every other layer, it seems) that the endless burning of fossil fuels is doing? As far as I can see, it is the basis for the global warming theories (not yet proven, I should add), and we are constantly told that we are all going to be fried, with our society and food supply destroyed.

It is an effective marketing campaign, to be sure, and the last thing the opponents of this cleansing idea want to see (assuming its principals are looking to grab ultimate power from this—also written about; look it up!) is for the atmosphere to be scrubbed clean, allowing us to go back to the start of the industrial age and live life (with fancy cars, no less) as we see fit.

I would also imagine the major oil companies, blinded with the need for ever higher bottom lines and dividends, would not be amused at a new and sudden burst of oil supplies being literally mined from the skies. It is not going to go anywhere, this "sky-cleansing," to give it a name; there is too much opposition. I just wanted you to be aware of what might be an excellent form of pollution control.

CHAPTER 8

How God Trades Oil! Money, First, Last, and Always – Why Your Pump Prices Have Been So High for So Long

Finally, I would like you to see how a major trader in the oil pits operates. He is nicknamed "God" and is rumored to work for either a major US bank or trading firm. See what you think!

One of the things I find so appalling is how US brokerage firms trade and encourage their clients to do likewise. They seem to have no idea what a trend is. One of the Rothschilds in Paris, about 150 years ago, said that the way to make money was to have an idea and let the market start to run with it. Then you buy in, with the trend most probably established, and observe what you were considering in the real world of financial markets. You watch it move, and when the market becomes overenthusiastic about the trend, you bail out.

This is how you should trade, and it should net you large profits with little risk—if you are any good at what you are doing. In a move from, say, 100 to 300 in a stock (which we assume is your idea), you should let the gamblers take the first forty points from 100 to 140 (or 20 percent of the entire proposed move). You step in and buy at 140, selling out at 260. The last 40 points you leave for all of the wild-eyed enthusiastic traders to overstay their welcome and ultimately get crunched as the inevitable correction occurs.

You can make serious money using this approach. You generally know you are correct if, when you sell, people are ridiculing you for selling "such an obvious money spinner" or some such. This is something I look for all the time.

What does the average American trader do? (This is why something like seventeen out of twenty lose money, with most of the rest breaking even.) He may have an idea that something is going to happen in a certain stock and buys it. Fine and dandy with that, but then one of two things will happen. First, he will see a decent gain in the first week or so and immediately take profits on the idea that "profits do not take themselves." This person then misses most of the rest of the move, waiting for a pullback to reenter the trade, which never comes.

The other possibility is that this person's idea is wrong and they will not admit it by selling out and taking a manageable loss, thereby ultimately losing most of their trading capital. They buy when their broker tells them to do so, and likewise sell. They make next to nothing, as just noted. They always think that losing money is "for someone else" and that "if I can just hang on I will be fine." In other words, I should never lose. *Please*, find me a market that operates on this principle!

The real trader is "God," to get back on track here. As far as I can tell, he is an experienced floor trader trading crude oil futures. He has sold his senior management on the idea that oil is going up and is going to go up quite a long way. He is looking at the fundamentals, which his board of directors is probably considering as well.

He looks at the market and sees endless backwardation, which is getting larger (i.e., the shortages are getting worse). He then looks at what the major countries are doing as regards oil, and he sees that the informed money in those places is telling him that oil is something to go after as fast as possible. (Of course, you have to be able to read what this informed money is saying and doing.)

For example, he sees Britain telling the Argentinian government to back off from its dubious clams to the Falklands archipelago, and is actually building a six-thousand-foot airstrip on the very remote island colony of St. Helena in the South Atlantic Ocean. This facility can be used, if the Argentines needed any further prodding on this score, as a military base if it was deemed necessary. Of course we then see that the Falklands are sitting on what could be a mother lode of oil!

He sees the possibility that the planners in the Kremlin have managed to bring Crimea back into Russian hands, with possibly huge supplies of oil and natural gas offshore. We have all read about how China is looking to threaten Indonesia, Japan, Taiwan, the Philippines, and now Vietnam with border claims in the South China Sea, where there is (surprise!) supposed to be vast oil deposits.

This goes on and on, with claims and counterclaims and the like in Mali (France's "former" colony) and the Sudan/South Sudan in Africa, just to name two more places. There is even scuttlebutt about the United States making eyes at

Canada, most probably because of the giant deposits in the tar sands.

In short, the fundamentals are bullish, and informed money is trying to grab all it can get. This should mean that oil has, realistically, no nearby ceiling as to how far it can advance. "God" then makes his case to his board of directors, who may be leaning the same way, and they agree to back him all the way on this one. He therefore has acquired billions of dollars in credit he can fall back on to meet margin calls and the like, and he trades aggressively. He starts to be noticed (as he should be) in the pits and attracts gasps of awe at what he is doing.

He acquires the blasphemous nickname of "God" because of his seemingly uncanny ability to turn markets in his direction and force less well-capitalized traders to cover their positions from him at a premium. Being a longtime trader myself, I can say that he trades in these tick-by-tick markets with an underlying idea of what oil should be doing at various levels because he understands these markets and what makes them go. His knowledge of the fundamentals is staggering, and it shows.

His board of directors can see him trade and what their returns are. They are clearly pleased and, needing all sorts of trading profits for their bottom line, they let him continue. Using Rothschild's dictum noted above, I believe it is very possible that while "God" trades in and out, leaving less well-capitalized traders (note: very important, you can't trade without capital) in the dust, he probably has a core position of contracts which he will not sell, and why should he?

If he currently holds these at an average entry price of, say, $85–90, he is well onside with a lot of padding in case something should go drastically wrong based on today's prices of $104 or so. He may well feel that oil will go to $150 or thereabouts, and this is his trading target. If he is correct about fracking's limited holding power, which I believe that he is, then on something like a holding of ten million barrels he is going to make his principals a profit of roughly $650 million, and that would be before any in-and-out trading profits are taken into consideration with technical adjustments on this core position. It is a nice chunk of money for the bottom line of a major financial institution that might be hurting these days.

What is the point of telling you how a corrupt system works, anyhow? It is simply to inform you how the current shortage of oil is recognized by some bright people, who are using it to make all sorts of money. The fact that you, the end consumer, are going to have to pay these profits (the $650 million comes from somewhere, after all) should tell you that oil and energy are in tight supply.

It should also tell you that any pullbacks at the pump in prices are going to be short-term and that you will see these price reductions reversed en route to ever-higher charges at future fill-ups. "God" and others of his kind are doing nothing to increase the supplies available for society, but they are making very sure that their pockets will be well lined for the day when governments around the world finally crack and have to tell their electorates that they are well and truly screwed.

By this time, the big hitters are going to be nowhere to be found and are long-since retired to a very nice existence. Thank you very much!

Well, now you know a little bit about the problems and possibilities (and the slippery politics) in the energy segment of the global economy. I have *not* included any comments about coal (of which the United States has a huge reserve in places like Wyoming), as it is such an easy target for environmentalists who roll their eyeballs when people mention coal or coal gasification as a way around the growing shortages of the biggie—oil.

Germans have a large quantity of brown coal in their country, but the powerful environmental lobby there is most displeased at the prospect of large amounts of atmospheric contaminant being released when it is burned. However, given that the EU government in Brussels seems determined to allow fracking in Western Europe (for whatever that is worth, given its limited shelf life), it would not surprise me to see brown coal-burning being allowed in greater quantities there, as well.

Have a good look at all of the bits and pieces I have put together here for you. Yes, you may disagree with some of them (Bedini Schoolgirl?), but that is fine. All I want you to do is to analyze what the underlying problems are going forward (there are many of them) and think about what all of this means to you and yours. Be aware, and think!

Now I must have a look at the underlying global politics in the last segment of this book, as this will also paint a picture (ugly, but a picture nevertheless) of what is driving many nations these days. How are the powerful reacting? What happens to the weak and defenseless? Let's find out.

SEGMENT 4

CHAPTER 1

Is the State Department Correct? Can Iran Start Throwing Nukes Around?

All kidding aside (and in all of my efforts to date I have tried, from time to time, to use the lighter touch a bit), we now have to sum up what has gone before in preparation for the final segment of this book. We have seen what I hope is interesting pi analysis from the Bible, which should make you wonder if what it forecast could be what some of the doomsdayers are calling for. In segment 2, we took a long look at what I sincerely believe lies ahead for Canada (and western Canada—ABC Land) against a voracious appetite for raw materials of a famished United States. Will the United States be able to "chomp, chomp" its way to fulfillment without having to devour her neighbors completely? Sadly, I do not think so.

In the last segment, we had what I think was a decent look at what constitutes many forms of alternative energy and why nearly all of them are failures and will probably soon be recognized as such. We could also, in this segment, have a look at something the Japanese are supposed to be interested in, and that is solar power with a twist.

According to the *Japan Times* this morning, Japan wants to launch a huge array of very large satellites that will capture the sun's rays and microwave them to Earth to be used as electricity to replace nuclear power. As I recall, this was discussed decades ago, and it was thought that it belonged in the realm of science fiction, and that was that.

However, no matter what you believe as regards alternative energy forms and their potential for adding to our staggering energy requirements, the fact remains that we are going to need lots of ways to generate power and cut back on the supposedly demonic use of fossil fuels. We have been looking at wind power, solar power, and allied items. The situation is not going to get any better what with people running around playing politics and always claiming that "we have the solution"—whether "we" is a nation or a company, big or small.

So what is the true state of affairs in the world? How have global societies constructed themselves for what is clearly the end game in power generation? The big question I have, of course, is *the question*. Way back in the first stages of this book, I wrote a rather flattering article on Marty Armstrong. Not that he doesn't deserve it, of course, but one of the points I raised was his discovery of the grisly war cycle, which comes to a twenty-five-year peak in 2015 (that's this year).

How will war affect the very delicate political and economic situation around the world? (*The question!*) We have to include the economic situation, of course, as what happens there can cause massive upsets in global derivative markets and the world's interest rate structure.

I cannot write about every nation, as I simply do not want to continue writing about the large number of societies existing on our globe and not be finished by next Christmas. There are several hot spots on our planet, and these will probably suffice because any real problems there will drag in the major powers with who-knows-what effect on everybody else.

The United States rants and rails against Iran and how it has developed nuclear weapons for use against its Arab neighbors. Iranians are *not* Arabs, by the way, and are Shi'ite Muslims versus the Sunni sects that largely dominate the entire region outside that country. Sunnis and Shi'ites hate one another with a rare passion, and one only has to think back to the sectarian troubles in Northern Ireland a generation or so ago, when Roman Catholics and Protestants came close to a civil war over this issue.

It was embarrassing for London (Northern Ireland is part of the UK), and the Vatican has been trying to bring the rival churches together for many years now. Nevertheless, Sunni-Shi'ite violence has happened, and so we can at least understand why various branches of a supposedly solid religion such as Islam can come to blows very easily.

Paul Craig Roberts writes a quite extraordinary series of newsletters most frequently these days and has written on the subject of Iranian nuclear weapons, quoting an amazing story from the *Afghan Times*. I wrote a long newsletter on this at the time. I would like to reproduce it for you now:

> Well, I have finally screwed up my courage and started to think seriously about something that

should not be—the Islamic Republic of Iran having a cache of nuclear weapons and what has happened around the world with that knowledge being clearly imprinted on so many diplomats' and leaders' minds. First see http://kabulpress.org/my/spip.php?article85229. Yes, this is a newspaper published in Kabul, Afghanistan, and at first I looked at the URL and winced.

I wondered about the sort of rubbish that might come out of that war-torn city, but as it was recommended by Paul Craig Roberts in his most recent letter of November 13, I felt I had to give it at least a look-see. I am glad that I did. This story, together with a large number of others referenced on the same page, contains more information than I had ever thought possible. Clearly there is no press censorship in Kabul! The authors seem to have a lot of knowledge based on previous life experience, and from what I know of the subjects being discussed, they are not wrong in what they write. See this cut from one of their subsidiary stories—Iran's nuclear weapons program:

EXCLUSIVE: Iran's Black Market Nuclear Warheads Are an Open Secret

They continue to restrain Western military action

Saturday 22 October 2011, by Matthew J. Nasuti

On March 21, 2008, this author was among a group of foreign service officers and diplomats who received a briefing at the State Department on Iran.

I can see the comments now: "Gerry, stop being such a chump. Isn't it obvious that anybody can write this sort of stuff? And in case you hadn't noticed, this is more than two years old." To this I merely state, "So what?" We are looking at a long-term trend here, which goes back decades to the time of the Shah of Iran, and it is quite conceivable that this *Afghan Times* article is just one of an ongoing series of updates.

However, what can be gleaned from this story is that the Western powers take their time to react, and so they have done in this instance. How many times have we seen "scary stories" about Iran doing devilish things with their enrichment programs? How many times has Israel cried for something to be done about this apparent wickedness in Tehran? How many times have we seen (well, I certainly have) stories that "within six months Iran will have a bomb"? Quite a few over the last decade, I would say. Let us continue with the newsletter on this very dangerous subject:

The West has reacted in several ways. First, they have slapped Iran with all manner of sanctions on its economy. Its oil cannot be paid for in USD, but that so far has not been that much of a burden overall. Secondly, there are all sorts of diplomatic sanctions in place. In the grand scheme of things (nukes versus everything else), these sanctions do not amount to much more then the proverbial hill of beans. How can they?

However, in following the money (my favorite system for assessing things, as it relies on greed and human nature, which never fail) we see that there are tell-tale signs that what Iran is doing *is* in fact the truth and that the *Kabul Press* is clearly privy to a great deal of information not widely disseminated in the Western press. What could these signs be?

Initially, the most obvious reason is that despite a huge number of threatened attacks on the Islamic republic, nothing definitive has ever been done. Why should this be so? Clearly, if Iran has nuclear weapons, an attack on that large country that did not get them all would invite a retaliation of some description.

This would not come in the form of a Shahab-4 missile aimed at London or Washington but rather at the oil fields of Saudi Arabia or the Middle East in general. Why shouldn't they react in this manner? I believe it was one of the Afghan leaders who came up with the idea that America cannot be beaten in a direct military showdown (most probably correct) but that the way to attack the United States would be its economy.

This could be done via staging a series of brushfire wars in central Asia (i.e., Iraq and Afghanistan), which would be waged using guerilla tactics. These would cost the United States a staggering amount of money. Looking at the overall US debt burden's increase in the past decade or so, this seems quite correct. If your enemy tells you how he is going to defeat you, why would you not pay attention?

If the prospect of your enemy doing a great more damage to your now-weakened economy via damaging your most precious import (oil), then you have a real worry on your hands. Overall, this in fact is quite a threat, and I am inclined to believe that Washington and the EU are not going to go too far down that particular path—that is to say, attacking Iran's nuclear weapons and risking a collapse in your overindebted, overleveraged economy.

It also explains something else that has been irritating me for some time now, and which I wrote about to an energy newsletter some time ago. In assessing this, in that letter, I was taken by the fact that all major discoveries were being guarded zealously.

In particular, with the discoveries of what may be mega-deposits in the Falkland Islands (which I have more than a nodding acquaintance with), London is going as far as building an airport on remote St. Helena Island in the South Atlantic, which could apparently handle military flights going south to Port Stanley/Mt. Pleasant in the Falklands. The short shrift given to wretched Argentina over the issue was most noteworthy. Why? I asked.

China has threatened to nearly come to blows with Japan over the riches of the South China Sea. China has also bought into the tar sands in Alberta, and I had considered this a normal asset play for its national balance sheet. Now the answers are clearer, and the money trail can only lead to the Middle East.

If the feeling in major global capitals is that Iran could really wreck the joint, then any and all discoveries anywhere will be guarded with great definition. Another way of putting this would be to say that these people are clearly in the know about what Iran is capable of, consider it a very real probability, and are hedging their bets all down the line. Argentina and Japan are, in all probability, going to be left out in the cold. Iran is that serious.

What else can we say? It is known that the United States is seriously considering establishing an anti-missile base in Poland. This was announced well more than a year ago, and the reason stated was that the EU would need it to protect itself from an Islamic Iran and a possible attack. The

EU was quite content with this, but not so the Russians. They seemed quite convinced that the proposed base was aimed at them, using the rather straightforward logic that an anti-Iranian base should be much closer to Iran than Poland.

What was interesting here was that despite all sorts of references to Russia eliminating this base along the lines of what President Kennedy threatened to do in the Cuban Missile Crisis in 1962, the United States refused to back down. There were a few small givebacks to placate the Russians, but the overall idea was unmovable: the United States will not back down.

So far, nothing of consequence has been heard from Moscow on all of this activity, but if President Putin is as closely linked with Iran as the West seems to think, then he knows full well what is happening and can only play the "wounded Russian pride" card for so long.

The United States was prepared to risk, in other words, a major confrontation with Moscow over what *is* (in my opinion) an anti-Iranian base. Therefore, we can conclude that the Iranian threat is very real and is perceived as so in Western capitals. They are panicking and are probably right to do so.

Why would this be, anyhow? The feeling in another edition of the *Kabul Press* is that Iran would have no scruples about selling these fiendish weapons to what the West calls terrorist groups. Has this happened, and are Iran and/or these groups engaging in all sorts of bluff and double-bluff with Washington these days? I do not know—at least a direct basis.

However, we can follow what is happening in Washington and see that the corridors of power there contain some truly frightened people. How do we know that? We simply look at what is happening in that country. Since the attacks on 9/11, we have seen a proliferation of security agencies develop there whose principal motive seems to be to find out absolutely everything that is written or spoken in the United States at any one time.

Why would this be in the United States, of all places? The only answer that makes sense is that Iranian nukes are now loose in the world, and as such the question can only be how many have been smuggled into the United States. What threats has Washington received that make American leaders react as they have? Surely there must have been some very nasty ones along the way.

Therefore, while many civil libertarians and right-wing bloggers are overtly hostile to TSA, DHS, and who knows what else, I am now thinking that they are wrong and that these new alphabet institutions really are devoted to stopping something awful from emerging in the United States.

Yes, there is a real problem with what might be called "mission creep" or the simple problem of senior bureaucrats looking to expand their empires before other agencies do. For instance, I see today that the EPA, in a desire to expand their mandate to protect American waterways, may even wish to impede the private ownership of property! So where is the EPA going with all of this?

It is not good and would ultimately result in state control of everything in the name of protecting the land, water, and, of course, people. I mention this because we have to look at how the TSA is expanding their remit from simple airport inspectors to possessing armored trucks and cars, which can patrol highways looking for possible terrorists. The DHS and the listening agencies have all been in the headlines recently, both home and abroad, spying on just about everyone (including the German Chancellor Merkel) to see what the terrorists are up to.

Where do they go from here? Just how serious is the Iranian threat, and does it justify this sort of mission creep (or should we call it mission gallop)? The right-wing blogs have been having a field day worrying that everything we are seeing has been put in place prior to some sort of takeover attempt of the entire United States by a major entity.

The motive here would be that taking over the United States would actually be saving it and making sure that it continues to exist as an independent entity safe from the Iranian threat. The same blogs have commented that Obama is overmatched in his job (and one can see this in his physical deterioration since he has been in office). What I think they are saying (and this may be nothing but rampant speculation on my part) is that in the current environment of an apparent failure of Obamacare, the Iranian threat, and the rapid growth of an all-encompassing bureaucracy, perhaps someone else could be found to take over this very demanding job.

It also appears that in the attempt to gain ever more control over their mandate, Washington agencies are looking to take advantage of many unfortunate incidents which have been happening. I refer to the Boston Marathon bombing, where two Chechen immigrants to the United States apparently set off a homemade bomb that caused many casualties.

The results in finding the one Chechen who eluded initial capture were that homes were searched in a systematic basis and the whole city was placed in a lockdown mode. Many Constitutionalists objected to what happened, but it seems to be a question of irrelevance. Bostonians did not object and in fact cheered the local police when the danger had passed.

This sort of civic reaction tells any and all who are watching that there is no problem for the average American in accepting additional bureaucratic encroachment, on the understanding that "it makes us all safe." There is to be no more boogeyman to imperil what Americans regard as their lifestyle, and that is the bottom line to all of this.

Given that, in the thrust of this letter, we are seeing a genuine fear of what a really dedicated terrorist could do with a rogue nuke in the United States, the federal authorities are going to have their hands full. They really cannot afford to have a small nuke (if one of these actually exists) explode in a major US city during, say, rush hour.

That would tell all and sundry that the alphabet agency clampdown is simply not working and that individual US citizens are not being protected. This may sound somewhat harsh, given that many Iranian bombs may have been tracked down and removed from US society, but one will be all it takes, what with the great veil of secrecy prevailing over the entire issue.

I would say, based on what has been written over the past few days, that if there is even one nuclear explosion in the United States, that there will be a complete clampdown on anything and everything in the country. It would be foolish to expect that the relevant agencies have not drawn up plans should this nightmare ever occur. It may even be that events outside US borders would be impacted as well.

One of the things I have done for many years now is research what the United States might do if it felt it needed to do so. On the US/Mexico border is a fence, and this is policed rather aggressively to stop Mexicans (and who knows who else) from coming into the United States proper. There have been articles showing that the US Border Patrol would like to have the authority to patrol within Mexico itself and to effectively control the area under a sort of *cordon sanitaire*. I do not think that this has happened or is going to happen anytime soon. However, if something disastrous happens in the United States courtesy of Iran, then all bets may be off.

In Canada (which has the so-called longest undefended frontier in the world with the United States) we see something similar. Some years ago, there was apparently some sort of exchange agreement between Canadian and American law enforcement to the effect that

US police officers from various states could patrol, with an RCMP escort, within Canada to a certain distance.

As far as I can recall, this must have been some sort of pilot program as it was only undertaken east of Vancouver, British Columbia. I cannot recall Canadian police officers patrolling south of the border, which is interesting. Canadian motorists were pulled over fairly routinely, and the whole practice wasn't formally exposed until one of the people being pulled over was an off-duty Vancouver police officer who apparently took exception to being ticketed by a Texas patrolman.

What is of great interest to me is that it does not seem to have been an agreement between governments, but rather between various national police forces only. The only logical conclusion one can make from all of this subterfuge was that there was a deeper purpose involved. In the light of what I have been writing, I conclude that this "agreement" was merely an extension of Washington police powers, and an extension that could well be used in a time of great emergency—an Iranian emergency.

Something along the lines of all of this was a cordon sanitaire reaching into Canada as well as Mexico. Old maps that I saw online suggest that the American authorities requested a 100-mile security buffer, which, as far as I saw, suggested that only the prairies would be affected. Later on this was reduced to fifty miles, but I have seen nothing further. Again (and this may be completely true in Alberta with the huge tar sands deposits—a rich prize if the Iran thing gets out of control) I wonder about these sorts of what might be regarded as extreme planning.

This is quite a lot of material for my readers to digest in just a few days. Looking at the quality of information in the *Kabul Press*, there may be other such analyses coming in the new year. You are probably tired of me saying this, but again, 2014/15 is the end of the twenty-five-year cycle—the war cycle of Armstrong, a correct theory in my view. Looking at what we have been discussing over the past week or so, why is it so unreasonable to expect that this war cycle will not play out as it has done often in the past?

It could be that all of the previous threats against Iran were rebuffed because it simply wasn't the time (cycle-wise) for such things to work. If that is so, then the mullahs in Tehran are going to have a big shock this time. It may be that the Saudis and the Israelis (now there's an unholy alliance for you) will attack initially with the United States picking up the residue (with all bills paid for by Riyadh; this is important for US budgetary reasons). This may be how it is presented to Washington, but in war things seldom go as planned.

We can confirm that the mess in Washington from an overmatched Obama (I suspect that virtually anybody else would have the same problem right about now) requires that the White House try something else. The GOP is running all over the place laughing at the inept rollout of Obamacare, but they miss the point.

The real problem in DC (which the leadership of the GOP should know all about, as it is a long-term difficulty) is Iran and terrorist groups with nuclear weapons. Right after this must be the very real problem with the budget and the quaintly American institution of the debt ceiling. These are critical issues, to be sure, especially the debt ceiling, and if the GOP leadership does not understand these things, we are all in trouble.

For Obama to go after a sideline/distraction war, he must market it properly to a jaded American public, and it must have something of real significance. Just look at the results of the Boston bombing noted above. It seems to me that Americans will sell their collective souls for a bit of short-term safety, and there are far too many people in Washington, DC, who are willing to give them what they want.

If a war in the critical Middle East is just one more nail in this particular coffin, then so be it. It will not be hard to get the public onside for such a conflict, especially if it is said that "the Saudis will pay for it all. There is no downside, and your safety will be assured." If there is any problem, then surely another so-called false flag will put the quietus to any opposition. There *will* be a war, in my view. The odds on it happening are simply far too high.

So this is quite a bit of information from a couple of articles in a Kabul newspaper! Look for more, as noted before, simply because there are so many knock-on effects to be considered once the calendar rolls into 2015.

Oh, one thing I forgot. If Iran *is* using old Soviet nukes, then an explosion in a US city can be blamed on the Soviets (nuclear radiation signature), which is convenient as the Soviet Union no longer exists. Iran could claim that they are "blameless" in such a tragedy, but I wonder how that would play out in Washington.

CHAPTER 2

Enough on Iran, Gerry! Okay, How Do You Feel about North Korea?

Let's ease into this a bit rather than hit you with a sudden change from Iran to the Democratic People's Republic of Korea (DPRK, or North Korea). The United States, if one reads literally any newspaper, has a *lot* of problems around the world. We have just had a long look at the intense problems that the United States has with Iran (wouldn't it be the ultimate irony if the United States was forced to join forces with Iran against the ISIL insurgency forces in neighboring Iraq?), and these are not going to go away at all.

Well, think about this. If you were Iran's rulers and were faced with a very hostile United States (not to mention Saudi Arabia), would you give up your nuclear weapons? I wouldn't, as they are probably all that are standing between a belligerent State Department and national annihilation. This is the big problem for the United States, and it may be insoluble given that the US planners generally have a rather narrow timeline on the decisions they make. (Act in haste, repent at leisure?)

To be frank, I have never been a fan of the US State Department and what it is trying to do overseas. However, I make a large exception when it comes to Iran. The overthrowing of the Shah of Iran (and the "Peacock Throne") in 1979 was seen in Iran as the elimination of the man the United States kept in power to make sure that Iran stayed firmly in the Western camp.

Ayatollah Khomeini put an end to that in double-quick time, and hatred of the United States there grew, culminating in the attack on the US embassy in that year as well. I do not believe that this attitude has changed, and the chant of the Revolutionary Guards—"Death to America"—is still current. The State Department is doing their job properly in the case of Iran, and if Iran *does* have nuclear weapons, Washington would be criminally remiss not to have sanctions and defensive postures just about everywhere.

One wonders about the price of oil and the Iranian nuclear threat. If Americans are groaning about gasoline prices with oil at its current (May 2014) level of $104, what do you think the reaction will be if Iran uses one of its nukes on Saudi Arabia?

Do you now see why I devoted a full segment of this book to assessing the merger between Canada and the United States? There are so many variables to be considered in the oil markets these days, not to mention COMEX market backwardations saying that we are in long period of shortages, that I do not believe these merger talks are going to go away.

The need for the United States to secure long-term supplies as quickly as possible is now paramount. It is entirely possible that the meeting of NAFTA heads of state in Mexico in February 2014 saw all of this laid before them in the simplest terms. Hillary Clinton, ever the opportunist, saw in this the possibilities of a much more integrated North American continent: Mexican labor, US manufacturing capacity, and Canadian natural resources. As I have mentioned many times in my newsletter, there are far too many interested parties for these merger talks not to continue on various levels.

We also have the problems in the Ukraine, which are not going to go away. It looks like Russian President Putin is playing a masterful game in the eastern part of that country. It looks to me that he is encouraging the Russian majority there to engage in a civil war with the Kiev government (which came to power in elections after a coup—Euromaidan, as we all saw in the newspapers).

The Ukraine is about as bankrupt as it is possible to get and is again finding problems in paying Russia for its natural gas, from what I understand. Putin is going to grind the United States and NATO down with endless low-intensity war while he goes after bigger game, probably in the Middle East.

The State Department is tied down in two places, therefore, and now we may see DPRK being a third. As you will see in this chapter, the United States may be realizing that it may have more on its plate than it can handle right now. It looks to be playing nice with Pyongyang (the capital and seat of power in North Korea), although there is a snag for Kim Jong-un's government there. What is this? Oh—perhaps the United States wants to eliminate DPRK by merging it with its southern neighbor?

As I have alluded to earlier, the year 2014/15 is a war cycle year—specifically the prime danger period in August of this year. So do we see a buildup in the Middle East because of the Iranian threat with an explosion shortly after this month? I see nothing to indicate that this is happening and, in fact, President Obama is looking to get peace feelers going with the Iranian authorities.

While many in the United States have condemned this "go soft" approach to Iran and favor something up to and including air strikes, this would be very bad indeed if there is a nuclear response. So, with this in mind, I do not favor the possibility of a United States-led attack on the country.

The other possibility is something that might be done in the Ukraine if Washington feels that it doesn't have what it wants after the May 25 elections there. However, the feeling I get in watching the financial markets is that there is not much to play for in the Ukraine—and in fact there never was, despite some rather bellicose statements made earlier on in the crisis.

Well, if we aren't seeing a war (or a major change of political structure, which is the other part of Armstrong's war cycle hypothesis), then what *do* we see? My favorite candidate is one that has not been seen discussed yet. In other words, there is no consensus as to what is to be done with the comical but very dangerous state of North Korea.

After Japan had its colonialist butt kicked in 1945, we have seen nearly seventy years pass—sixty-nine years, in fact—and this timeline will be complete in August. Now, sixty-nine is a pi cycle number, as is 2014, interestingly enough. My bet, therefore, is that something rather extraordinary is about to happen in North Korea. I have been assessing this for quite some time now, and my feeling is that the question of oil will once again lead the way.

I was told by a gentleman on a site I post to that the United States was in Vietnam because gobs of oil exist near the Chinese border. Today (well, in May 2014 anyway) we see the Chinese threatening to attack that area of Vietnam because of poor treatment meted out to Chinese tourists. In reality, I wonder. The United States was not able to grab Vietnamese oil reserves in the long war it suffered there, and now what about China?

The United States bears little love for Kim Jong-un's regime in Pyongyang. It has piled sanction on top of sanction with the usual sanctimonious words: "The international community is outraged at this, that, and so." This is usually in response to a nuclear test of some sort, and Pyongyang merely shrugs off Washington's sense of "outrage." However, unlike Washington's genuine irritation with Tehran, there usually seems to be a bit of carrot to go along with the stick aimed at Kim.

I keep asking myself why this is the case, and recently I found out what may be the reason: oil. Off the east coast of DPRK, there seems to be a fair bit of deep-sea oil that has not been touched because Pyongyang does not have the technology. Off the west coast, there has been no attempt to develop oil reserves in the North's share of Korea Bay. China has no problems in developing their side of this waterway (and the connecting others), so I do not accept the idea that there is nothing there for North Korea. Oil deposits do not generally recognize international boundaries.

So how does the United States get its energy-starved mitts on this oil? Well, we have to have some idea of what is going on in that very opaque corner of the world. I have studied it since 1983, and I wish to attach my newsletter comments (well, some of them, anyhow) for your interest:

> I chanced to read in this morning's *Daily Telegraph* (London) a really interesting story about the future of North Korea and what various powers seem to be doing about this. A large number of question marks that have been hanging over this "reclusive Stalinist state" (to use the usual method of the Western press in describing this rather bizarre country) are now, to my way of thinking, being resolved. Have a look at this article quotation: "China has drawn up detailed contingency plans for the collapse of the North Korean government, suggesting that Beijing has little faith in the longevity of Kim Jong-un's regime."[6]
>
> In looking at this information along what I have been following from *Chosen Ilbo*, the *South China Morning Post,* and the *Japan Times* (all of which have good connections, shall we call them, with senior Chinese leaders), we can now probably surmise some quite plausible answers to most of the following questions about the comings and goings in Pyongyang.

---

6   Julian Ryall, "China Plans for North Korean Regime Collapse Leaked," *Daily Telegraph,* May 5, 2014, http://www.telegraph.co.uk/news/worldnews/asia/northkorea/10808719/China-plans-for-North-Korean-regime-collapse-leaked.html.

1) Why was Kim Jong-un's uncle, Jang Song-Thaek, executed very rapidly after a show trial that was a mockery even by their loose standards?

2) During this "trial," why was Kim a long way from the danger area in Pyongyang, apparently inspecting a very remote military base on the DPRK border with China?

3) Why has *Chosen Ilbo* been running on its front page, until very recently, a series of articles about possible Korean reunification?

4) Why was it that US Secretary of State Kerry visited Beijing in April 2014, with reunification on the docket for detailed talks?

5) Why has the US policy toward DPRK been one of sanctions, but very loosely enforced, when other countries around the world have felt the full weight of Washington's wrath in this regard? The answer to this will be fairly obvious as you read on and think about it. Washington wants a reunified Korea, and if a bit of carrot-versus-sanctions stick is the way to go ... well, why not?

6) Why did Beijing allow such a sensitive document to be "leaked" to a Japanese newspaper at a time of fairly intense strain in the relationship between the two countries?

7) Why has the DPRK leadership turned fairly hostile toward its one benefactor, China?

These are good questions, and if we put the answers together, I think we can see what lies ahead in Northeast Asia. I am not sure that I can answer all of them, but I think I can give you enough on the rest so you can draw some conclusions of your own. Not to forget our old friend the pi-cycle principle (to emphasize this yet again, as it may hold the key for stability throughout the world), we can see that since the Japanese were driven out of their Korean colony at the end of WWII, we have seen nearly sixty-nine years elapse.

The numbers 69 and 2014 are both pi-cycle numbers, and 2014 is also on Marty Armstrong's war cycle set of dates. So my conjecture is— and I have not abandoned this even though the attention of most of the world's media has been focused on Ukraine recently—that Korea is the place to be this year. If there is not going to be a war, then a massive change in how things happen in that area of the world look to be imminent. (Well, at least in this year!) This would also fit the possible outcome of a war cycle change, as it would be quite substantial, in my view.

Now we can see that questions (1) and (2) above have a decent answer. In both cases, and I wondered this at the time, it was quite likely that there was a coup underway or forthcoming in Pyongyang. Kim's uncle, the respected Jang Song-thaek (who many people suspected was really running the show in DPRK, with young Kim Jong-un as some sort of figurehead) simply didn't have the confidence in the Kim bloodlines, especially with a thirty-year-old at the helm. Kim was made aware of this and had Jang hauled out of the North Korean Parliament, dragged into a show trial that set records for speed, and then shot immediately.

Pictures released of Kim after all this was over showed him looking shocked and stunned at what had happened and what he had had to do. This makes sense if there was a coup about to be undertaken. One does not want to have your potential successor hanging around when the very balance of power was in flux.

Jang was "convicted" (depending on where one reads the events) of either womanizing or speculating with and illegal delivery of North Korea's plentiful supply of raw materials to Beijing. As this seems to have been part of his remit, it seems that his fate was unduly harsh, so there was probably something rather more substantial at stake.

If one now looks at Kim's official itinerary at the time of these rather nasty happenings, we see that he was well out of harm's way at a military base on the Chinese border—a rather remote base, I understand. If things had gone badly for poor old Kim, then he would have had protection and would not have had far to flee to the relative sanctity of China itself.

Interestingly enough, if we read the *Telegraph* article, we see immediately that the entire contingency plan to house fleeing North Korean leaders and VIPs comes from China. That apparently fits rather well. When Jang had been dispatched and the coup leadership did not have the strength to carry on, only then did Kim return to Pyongyang. In the following weeks, a lot of Jang's followers (read: fellow coup plotters, or a new government-in-waiting) also met Jang's fate.

Now let's look at questions (3) and (4). I watched Kerry's visit to Beijing (and reported on it in the newsletter at the time), and I saw precisely nothing. Now, clearly Kerry would not make a long visit to China unless he had something to say or wanted to understand the thinking of the Beijing leadership. Ultimately, some sort of cover story was released that said zilch in a high-sounding manner.

The South Korean newspapers, which had been fairly excited about reunification—for obvious cultural reasons—stopped their reporting on this. I do not think Pyongyang was pleased with what they were told was happening, as they proceeded to have a lot of "military exercises" that involved firing of many missiles into the ocean not that far from South Korean waters. So the lesson one takes away from this must be that something is being prepared by Beijing as far as its longtime pain-in-the-neck neighbor is concerned. The question is whether the United States was complicit in all of this, or would be complicit.

A reader was kind enough to write in and wonder about the *Telegraph* article. He wondered if a giant quid pro quo was in the works whereby China would let DPRK collapse and be absorbed into South Korea. The result of this would allow the United States—through its puppet in South Korea—full access to the Chinese border at the Yalu River.

It would be quite a prize for the United States, and in turn the United States would either allow Taiwan to be reabsorbed into China (a goal of Beijing ever since 1949) or else possibly stick it to the Japanese by recognizing China's claims to all of the oil and mineral resources in the South China Sea. In either event, it would be a win-win, and it may be that this reader is well up on his analysis. I commend his thinking along these lines. However, has the United States tried a double-cross? Yes, I think they have.

The *Telegraph* article says that China is preparing for the possibility of having millions of North Korean refugees streaming across the DPRK/China border into a portion of China with a good number of ethnic Koreans already living there. As I understand it, many of these Koreans are not overly fond of the leadership in Beijing and would like to rejoin their countrymen in a new sort of Greater Korea somehow.

They are what is called restive, in terms China has used to describe other areas of its vast country, say its far west region. Therefore, we can say that inner Mongolia and northeast Manchuria are vulnerable, especially if five to ten million North Korean refugees settle there.

I think the Beijing leadership has come to the conclusion that if the United States (as per the *Telegraph*) wants to foment something in North Korea that could cause its collapse, then the State Department has also planned for destabilization of China as a whole by having them absorb a huge number of hungry and desperate people. With China's financial institutions having a tough time right now with increasingly large numbers of bad real estate loans, having ten million desperate Koreans to worry about is not what China wants.

The United States would love to see all this, of course, and Beijing has probably realized that the entire US plan is lose-lose for them. They are angry, in other words, and they realize that if the United States starts some sort of action that results in the collapse of the Pyongyang government, it will be the Chinese who will have to clean up the mess—and it will be a big one! And what of Pyongyang? What do they think of all of this, especially as they will be front and center?

They know, I think, and are angry. The North Korean press has reported that in a visit to the country's primary military academy for officer training candidates, Kim told a class that they should regard China as their enemy now. This apparently caught the academy's commanders unawares, but they just happened to have the politically correct banners around from the last time (quite some time ago if I remember correctly).

Now why, out of the blue, did Kim make a speech like this? The obvious conclusion is that he is aware of what is happening behind the scenes and is furious. He is being sold down the river and knows it.

So what does he do going forward? My guess is that he fires off his fourth nuclear test (however that is configured). When both China and the United States are royally annoyed with him, he may actually initiate a war with South Korea, which would be ruinous for both halves of the Korean peninsula, and because of the way global economies are interlinked, the damage would reverberate across the world.

Don't forget that South Korea has the world's tenth biggest economy, and one does simply not remove this from the global economic equation without a lot of really bad things, possibly catastrophic things, happening. Is this what the United States might wish to see so that some sort of plan could be put into play that would cause widespread disaffection with the Kim regime? It is possible, although to try and calculate how all of this may play out with refugee flows into China is beyond me.

And what can we make (and extrapolate) from all the news from around the world today, and how it might all fit? I suspect the Japanese Prime Minister, Shinzo Abe, has more than an inkling of North Korea's impending demise, and this may be the reason why he is using every trick in the book to evade the Japanese constitution's ban of the use of the military abroad. In other words, if the United States cannot respond to what Kim is doing with North Korean forces, then maybe it can count on Japanese troops, although I think both halves of Korea would be revolted to see the troops from their former colonial overlord back again.

Abe will succeed, in my view, with his verbal sophistry. The Japanese constitution allows the use of the military for Japanese security, so Abe is saying that Japanese troops can be used for collective security—other close-by nations together with Japan. He is being painted as a latter-day warmonger, but the truth as I see things is a lot deeper than that.

Lastly, we must look at what the United States has done to its relationships with China. The Chinese appear to distrust Washington, and now that they read (and understand through many diplomatic channels, I would imagine) how Washington started the whole mess in the Ukraine (see Paul Craig Roberts' massive works on this sorry subject), they wonder if they are being set up to fail.

If they see Russia having trouble in its own backyard, then they must wonder if something similar was planned for them what with perhaps ten million Korean refugees streaming into northeast China. The communist government in Beijing shares a deep distrust (with other now-departed communist governments) about instability. They know they have troubles with their banks and vastly overextended balance sheets. They know their banks could easily topple and fail quite easily, and they simply do not trust what Washington may be up to.

It is probably something in this vein that has indicated that Beijing and Moscow have agreed to become close friends: they both now realize that they have a common enemy in Washington. How far this friendship will go will probably be seen when President Putin visits Beijing later on this month.

This is a fair amount of detail, and there is more—quite a bit actually. But I shall try to keep this down to something which will not bury you in minutiae (well, not too deeply, in any event). In order to understand more fully what is going on in DPRK, we must look at what the United States wants to do globally.

As we have been detailing in this book, the search for oil or something that can be used as a substitute (and which is politically acceptable) is intense. The United States has not been that harsh, when all is said and done, with the regime in Pyongyang, and I suspect that the State Department has its eye on what I believe are decent-sized oil fields on both of DPRK's coasts. That would say a great deal about global oil supplies.

The main thing I am looking at is that the United States may want a go-slow approach to dealing with the Kim government because it wishes to transfer the thirty-five thousand US troops in South Korea to other areas of the world—say, the Middle East, or possibly to NATO command in Eastern Europe to make a strong statement to Russia's President Putin.

So how can the United States basically emasculate North Korea and remove it from American worries as to how northeast Asia progresses? In recent months, there has been strong talk which may point toward some sort of Korean reunification—that is to say, having the North and South get together under one government (Korean, and not a colonist regime under one form or another) and to having a reunified Korean Peninsula for the first time in a *very* long time.

US Secretary of State Kerry has been making comments such as these, and there are happenings in the North which indicate that things may be underway to that effect. Predictably, the North is incensed at all of this (and they apparently feel that China may have sold them out on this issue), and there are two comments from the North Korean official press, *Rodong Sinmun*, on all of this. There is clearly a sense of anger at what the United States may (or may not) be doing to DPRK.

In an amazing article in *Rodong Sinmun*, the gloves came off in describing Barack Obama in a manner that would have done the old Ku Klux Klan proud. Comments about "the black monkey" and half-breeds not even belonging in a zoo were bandied about.[7]

These passed the official censor there, remarkably, and therefore reflect some really pent-up frustration on the part of the senior Party members in Pyongyang. This sort of language is simply not used in any sort of official communiqué, even one which goes through the press. The US reply to this was, equally remarkably, moderately restrained. There was the usual condemnation and a sort of "tut-tut, what *are* you

---

7   Chad O'Carroll, "President Obama a 'Wicked Black Monkey'— North Korean State Media," *NKNews.org*, May 8, 2014, http://www. nknews.org/2014/05/president-obama-a-wicked-black-monkey-north-korean-state-media.

people doing," but that was all. No follow-up at all, and I was looking for it.

My best guess is that Washington knows fully well the reason for this outburst. Washington and Beijing have probably come to an arrangement to finally muzzle North Korea permanently. They are going to do this, according the *Telegraph* in London (a nice leak), via a unification of North and South. There have been several articles in leading South Korean newspapers (e.g., *Chosen Ilbo*) wondering about how the society of South Korea would be changed by such a merger. So a merger between the two halves of Korea and a possible merger between the two halves of North America could both be in the cards! What next? I wonder.

Rodong Sinmun also has another story that seems to be based on the reunification idea. As just noted, there was a story in the *Telegraph* of London to this effect, but it was couched in a more opaque format of "foreign intervention to destabilize the North," which would lead to its collapse. North Korea was furious when the president of South Korea picked up on this in a visit to Berlin (how appropriate, to give a Korean unification speech in a country which, until under a generation ago, was also divided along political lines). We saw the following commentary:

> The ghost-like watchword "gaining a great opportunity of unification" is afloat in South Korea these days.

> Park Geun Hye is making much fuss about getting ready for "unification" and "forming a preparatory committee for unification,"

talking about "gaining a great opportunity of unification" whenever a chance presented itself.[8]

The days of North Korea now appear to be numbered, and it is a question (always remembering that this year, 2014, is a war cycle year) that is going to keep Kim Jong-un and his entourage awake for many nights, I think. Yes, DPRK is what the West might refer to as a royal pain in the ass, without question, it seems to me. Is it as though it is "being handled"? Whether Kim and his regime appreciate what is happening or not, I suspect that DPRK's one clear friend, China, may be about to dump them. In a visit of a North Korean military academy recently, Kim made the astonishing speech that "China is now our number-one enemy." Hmmm … with friends like these!

---

8   "*Rodong Sinmun* Comments on Park Geun Hye's 'Doctrine of Gaining Great Opportunity of Unification,'" *KCNA*, May 8, 2014, http:// kcnawatch.nknews.org/article/bcu8.

CHAPTER 3

The Population Problem—There Are Not Enough of Us! Get Breeding, Y'all

Now we must leave the unusual country of North Korea and head toward a more significant story: that of the global population problem. No, this is not what you might think. This is a story of the *lack* of people who are apparently *not* clogging our globe and why this unusual circumstance is going to cripple the economies of the West and, by extension, the rest of the world before we are all too much older.

Let us commence with the island nation of Singapore, which is where I started to assess what was really happening (following, as is always the case, the money). A couple of years back, quite recently given the grand timeline under consideration, I read an article in a major Singaporean newspaper.

It mentioned that the government there was looking at the population growth of that small island nation (it is about three and a half times the size of the District of Columbia) and did not like what they saw. Yes, there were looking at a rise in population, in line with most of the rest of the world, but it was the wrong type! The fertility rate in that nation was a minuscule 0.79. What does this mean, in plain English?

It means that women are simply not producing children at anything like the rate that is needed for a strong, economic, and sustainable population. Let's look at this slightly differently. A man and a woman marry and decide to have a few children. In order to be able to replace themselves, these new parents must produce just over two children. The actual number, as far as I can see, is 2.1 children. They have to produce offspring so that when they die, there are two more people to replace them. We allow for accidental deaths and so forth, and this is why we arrive at two children plus the 0.1 for the accidents.

Zero population growth aficionados claim that if a couple has no children they are doing their part in slowing global population. This is a very superficial way of looking at things because it does not allow for economic considerations and a massive change of population not that many years down the road. The problem of Singapore (and this is true with many other nations around the globe) is that the population they have now pretty well guarantees an economic collapse.

Because Singaporean women do not produce children in anything like the normal replacement rate as held by fertility rate theory, the number of elderly people will continue to grow in relationship to the number of people working and producing goods, services, and taxes. With more and more people demanding services for the elderly and the pension payments that go with them, who is going to provide all of the required funds?

Confucian tradition demands that the elderly be treated with respect and care, and in Singaporean society this *will* be honored. But how is this to be done? The planners in Singapore have decided that their population will have to be *increased,* and the only way is to encourage a lot of new immigrants and workers to come to this crowded island nation and work.

If the elderly stop working because of their advancing years, who is going to replace them at their productive jobs? There are no local candidates for the numbers required, and so the immigration barriers are going to come down. The population will be allowed to increase to well more than 7 million from the current level of 6.3 million or so.

This will cause a problem with already high-priced housing, and so the government is going to continue to reclaim land from the sea and use this to build new apartment blocks and the like for the new arrivals. Yes, there will be (as noted) an increase in population, but so what? When the older Singaporeans start to die off (and they will, along with the co-aged in every other country across the world), then the population, because of the current imbalances, will start to nosedive.

The zero population growth people are going to be able to claim victory, and that is fine by me (but please read on). It reflects the collective decision by Singapore's women not to have children in any quantity whatsoever. If that is what they want, which must mean in extremis the end of Singaporean civilization, then their wombs have spoken, and spoken loudly. However, women are unlikely to do this sort of thing without a solid reason, and in numerous articles we are seeing why: the economy.

If major corporations are so desperate to squeeze every last penny out of society to feed their already-bloated shareholders, then they will doom that society completely. If they are so hell-bent on keeping wages and benefits as low as possible and keeping taxes equally low to boost their collective bottom lines, there will be consequences. These consequences are that people will not be able to buy any sort of longer-lasting home security or even planning for a home, because the economy is too "iffy."

Why sign on to a long-term mortgage when it is highly likely that you will be laid off or fired from your job (by no fault of your own, just corporate greed and indifference) with who knows what results to your home and family? Do you wish to bring a lot of children (or even one or two) into this world when you may not be able to care for or raise them because of avoidable economic concerns?

This is not just me chattering away and causing you to reach for your Dramamine. This is what women in Singapore, Japan, and Korea are doing en masse. They do not have confidence in what lies ahead, and so they defer, often for far too long, to try having a family. Fertility rates are low in these three countries, and we are going to see the effects of this for some time to come. Would you like some more proof? Have a look at what I wrote in my newsletter about France recently:

> There is a template for this population crisis, and it is to be found, in the main, in today's France. In looking at the ruin of the EU's economy (and that is not just me saying this, just read virtually any comments on the overall mess it is in), we do

see that one country—a major one, France—has kept up its fertility rate to a hair under the 2.1 replacement level.

Women there are not afraid to have children, as the social benefits are large and continuing. Schools are made easy to enter, and in some cases an apartment in Paris (an apparently prized possession in France) can be made available. In other words, the economic uncertainties that are seen in so many countries have been ameliorated to such an extent in France that women are willing to have what may still be regarded as a traditionally sized family. The result is that with a steady fertility rate, France will not have the problems seen in the Far East, North America, and in much of the EU.

The supposed trouble with France is what shortsighted economic publications trumpet over and over again. These periodicals talk about "punitive tax rates" and "unwelcome state intervention in the economy."

Well, you asked for all of the problems that are now surfacing with rights issues in the past decade or so, and now that the fertility rates are coming home to roost, you complain. French bosses are crying at the restrictive laws on the books, which make firing people quite difficult. They say that there is no future to investing in France because the tax regime is so bad. The only way, they say, is to invest outside the country in an overseas subsidiary where the margins are good.

They say, they say, and yet the main Paris stock index, the CAC-40, is up more than 55 percent in the last two and a half years! What a mess, they say, and yet people think enough of what is happening there to buy French equities for large portfolios. I suspect that the crying and stamping of little French feet is due to the inability of French managers to do what they want compared to what they could do in other countries.

When a French billionaire moved himself and his money to neighboring Belgium not that long ago, the outcry was deafening. My question at the time was more basic. If France is such a dreadful place to live and invest, how did this man become a billionaire in the first place?

So French women are not afraid to conceive and, virtually alone in the major industrial countries of the EU, have kept their birth rate at the break-even point of just under 2.1 children per woman in their lifespan. So major industrialists and free marketers have been complaining in the most derisive terms that the French government is paying French women to have children and that this is the most intrusive of government policies in general.

Well, if French companies and those of the West in general are essentially stopping French women from having children by making the whole process so difficult and uncertain, what do they expect? Do they expect the French government to lie down and do nothing while their generally vibrant society slowly withers and dies?

The companies, therefore, have a choice. They can pay high taxes and make laying off expectant parents very difficult and have the French authorities react as they do, *or* they can pay decent wages and benefits and encourage women to have children, as there is a decent chance that they can raise their families without the excesses of modern capitalism. Companies cannot have it both ways, and the proof of this lies in collapsing birth rates globally.

However, Western governments in general still specialize in shooting themselves in the economic foot in trying to be all things to all people all the time. Let me now open up (a tiny crack!) the issue of women's rights in all of this.

For about a generation now, we have seen the idea that women, in general, should have equal rights in obtaining managerial positions through the national industrial spectrums. In their efforts to bend over backward as quickly as possible for all concepts that suddenly arise, governments laid down with breathtaking rapidity rules and regulations for women to be treated with extraspecial kid gloves.

We saw what follows in Japan, to a large extent, and we shall return to this benighted nation shortly. What happened? Women had an agonizing decision to make. Do they have a family, or a career that would bring in a lot of extra money into their households? As might be expected, they tried to have it all and wound up exhausted, trying to be a high-powered executive as well as a mother. Daycare centers (essential in a case such as this, I would have thought) became quite prevalent and now cost money that cannot be far off what the mother might be making in the workforce herself.

So why do it? The maternal drive is so strong that women simply did not want to give up having children altogether, and this was fortified when corporations started to realize that families now had two wage-earners and therefore a great deal more spending power. It was also realized that these same families could take a significant financial hit (e.g., a layoff because a job was sent overseas).

Women, exhausted from trying to have it all, simply cut back on the number of children they were conceiving. Fertility rates suffered accordingly, and now governments are saying a collective "oops" and are wondering what they can do. Let us stick with the Asian continent for a while and look at its major industrial power, Japan.

Japan is an island nation, in more ways then one. When I was much younger, I used to hear the word inscrutable used to describe how the Japanese live and work, and in my mind this still holds true. The nation is small, land-wise, at something a bit smaller than 60 percent of the size of Alberta, my home province (which, for my American readers, is slightly smaller than Texas). Into this smallish land area is squeezed 125 million people, versus just four million in Alberta.

In other words, the big cities in Japan (Tokyo comes to mind) are *really* big. Greater Tokyo has about forty to forty-five million people in it, which places it at the biggest in the world. Of course, if you live in that giant metropolis, you are living cheek-by-jowl with a lot of other people and are living in small and very expensive accommodations.

For many decades now, the Japanese economy was the second-largest in the world, after the United States, of course. It has now slipped into the number-three slot after China. It was (and remains, to be honest) a major industrial powerhouse, and the stories of the Japanese "salary man" putting in twenty-hour days was legendary. However, what wasn't asked at that time was how the wife of such a Japanese employee lived. What did she do in their shoebox-sized apartment, and was this any way to bring up the next generation?

I cannot believe it was, as the Japanese women jumped at the chance to make something of themselves when the American ideals of women's rights took hold. Japan, despite this idea, it is still a very much male-oriented society, and if a woman tries to advance herself within her company, she must not get married or else will find a very solid glass ceiling over her head.

The idea here is that if a woman gets married, she may well start to have children that would distract her from her all-important work at the company. Therefore, marriages are down, and so are the births of children. The fertility rate in Japan is bigger than that of Singapore, but at 1.3 to 1.4, it is still far below the replacement rate of 2.1.

Some months ago, in the excellent British newspaper the *Guardian*, there was a superb article about Japanese families and why they are not likely to see any sort of increase in the foreseeable future. I wrote a number of newsletter articles on this sorry state of affairs, and I wish to reprint them now for your ready reference:

> In recent letters, I have been assessing global population levels and found them to be less than satisfactory as regards the economic future of

mankind. I have discovered that not too many people agree with me, and that is fine by me!

In short, while population levels are high, most of the "too high" crowd seems to forget that the internal makeup of various ethnic populations is now tilted toward the aging side. This clearly shows that within a few years we are going to see substantial die-offs and consequent reduction of overall national populations. Now, if one considers that if the young (what there are of them!) are antipathetic toward breeding on any level, then we should have a situation to gladden the heart of any ZPG advocate.

Such a situation is now occurring in Japan as we speak. On the just noted article in the British newspaper the *Guardian* recently, we see that some 45 percent of sixteen- to twenty-four-year-old Japanese women abhor sexual contact of virtually any description. For the men, this works out to about 25 percent, which is also traditionally high. The implications of all of this are astonishing. What are we to make of this in a population whose fertility rate is 1.3, last I saw (and most likely dropping)?

When one combines that with a central bureaucracy that apparently does not care one jot about all of this, the stage must be set for something catastrophic for Japan. This same bureaucracy also has put out figures showing that by the far-off year of 2060, Japan's elderly will be a very large population relative to the youngsters.

Given that these numbers were probably compiled in 2010 (leaving a fifty-year window), we see a bureaucracy basically saying that this is a problem that will have to be taken care of in a very distant time. Being a practical person myself, I merely note that last year the sales of Japanese adult diapers exceeded those for infants for the first time. That is what you should be considering, in my view!

The story is some months old and comes under the heading of Japanese shunning sex. I strongly suggest you find and read it—long but worth it. I spoke to someone I know who made the acid comment that we can forget the fifty-year projections noted above. The damage to Japan will have been done in ten years, and possibly as little as five (given that trends are usually very tough to reverse, especially one such as this). The bottom line must be that if women do not wish to have children born into the nation of which they are such an integral part, then that nation dies. It is rather simple.

My own particular beliefs are that we can choose the body and the nation into which we incarnate (subject to one's personal karmic balances). Therefore, Japanese women being born into

Japan now apparently feel no compunction in keeping the population on an even keel in their chosen homeland. In other words, they are Japanese by choice but feel no burning desire to keep Japan going by breeding the next generation.

Well, if women will not perform, and with the traditional Japanese reticence at allowing large-scale immigration not having been reduced to any extent, Japan looks like a doomed society—probably a lot sooner than most people expect.

In the *Guardian* article, we see many reasons trotted out as to why children are not be born into that country. Basically, they revolve around women having good jobs and not wanting to have a boss fire them (in theory as opposed to practice) because they became married, with a probable pregnancy to follow at some point. The other reason will be much more difficult to fight: cultural exhaustion. The article mentions exhaustion several times. With endless problems in trying to raise a household and the children that invariably accompany such an enterprise, the effort required is apparently deemed not to be worth it.

It is too much investment of emotion for little return. The cost of living is very high, and Japanese women do not feel like having to work at a glass-ceilinged job and then return home to look after their residence. The person I spoke to, whom I mentioned earlier, made me aware of another possibility: Fukushima.

I have written regarding this nuclear atrocity, which is now well over three years old and not only shows no sign of being resolved but actually may even be getting a great deal worse. No less an American political authority such as Paul Craig Roberts feels that the radiation from the crippled nuclear reactor has by now seeped into the ground waters that provide drinking water for metropolitan Tokyo, and then when all is said and done, some fifty million people may be at risk.

I would imagine that there are many such stories circulating in that area of Japan, and so what is a young woman to think? The simple reply is that it is not worth the trouble of raising a family, that Japanese society has played itself out, and that there is no point in even trying to be a heroine and buck a clear trend.

This is not just Gerry Agnew making wild comments. In the last five years, Japan's population has declined in each year, from 130 million to 126 million. So, in this environment, where are the nation's leaders? Where are Prime Minister Abe and his very voluble deputy prime minister? What are they saying and doing?

Well, Abe seems to be interested in worshipping Japan's military ancestors (and infuriating his Korean and Chinese neighbors) at the Yasukuni Shrine, and his deputy has more than once called on simple elimination of the "tube people" (his term for older Japanese who are in nursing homes and riddled with feeding tubes and so forth to keep them alive).

I suppose that is one way of looking at things, as it *would* free up quite a few younger Japanese workers from taking care of the elderly, making them available for more profitable, export-led jobs. He assumes that once a worker stops intubating the elderly, the worker will quickly shift over to loading export ships and so forth. Not too bright, that assumption, I think!

Perhaps 25 to 40 percent of workers could be retrained for such work, and then what about the rest? We can also go a step further and wonder about the upcoming flood of retirees from the postwar generation. Will the Abe government want to kill them all as well? However, the die has now been cast here.

I am willing to bet that as more and more Japanese jobs become open because of retirement and possible emigration to the United States under its new immigration initiative, we shall start to see, in the leading Japanese newspapers, a call for a cull of the elderly (euthanasia, in other words). This would save the Japanese Treasury a lot of money and have distressed pension funds jumping for joy.

And what of less extreme measures? Abe has been trumpeting new daycare center initiatives and new deals for working women, to which I merely wonder just what token measures (given Japanese society) will be announced. Remember that it will be the women of Japan who will be the final arbiters of such attempts to write solutions to something which may be completely insoluble. As an economist, I simply wonder just how Abe is going to find the money to afford anything like such programs, which have proven to be so expensive elsewhere in the world. Let us have a look-see at what capitalism and socialism have to say about such things.

Initially we can look at France, which is being pilloried by just about everybody for daring to show the world a GDP which is comprised of about 57 percent government spending. The same articles also tell us that most major French companies now have about 90 percent of their sales overseas and that this is the norm in France, where it makes no real sense to carry on business. The unspoken word is that things have got to change there, but is this correct given the window through which we are looking—population growth?

I think not! If we look at the "liberated" world of unbridled capitalism, we see fertility rates of 1.2 in Korea, 1.3 (estimated) in wretched Japan, 1.4 to 1.5 in the EU, and 1.5 to 1.6 among the all-important white population in the United States (which I have been told is key to this nation's problems). Greedy corporate bosses (to quote so many columnists) are grabbing all they can for short-term benefits because, as we all know, the future is always some distance off and never something to be concerned about. Not this time.

Now we come to France and its "silly" system of internal free spending by the central government. Here we see a fertility rate of right around 2.1. I had to check this twice to make sure it was correct! In other words, while most other spendthrift nations are looking at disaster not that far down the road, France can look forward to the future with confidence.

Yes, there is always the problem of emigration to other EU countries, but on balance, France with its free family spending is fine. What all this says (and it is fairly easy to corroborate) is that France spends a lot of money on children and families. This seems to be a hangover from the 1870–71 Franco-Prussian War, when it was held that the reason why France lost was that it simply did not have enough people to be able to stem the Germanic hoards. This hit such a nerve that even today France is always frightened of not being able to have enough people to stem some future disaster.

After this brief revisit to France, let us return to Japan and North America for a quick look-see. In the *Guardian* article noted before, we saw a comment to the effect from one of the females being interviewed about what Abe was trying to do with daycare centers and so forth. She was not that impressed and said that the burden of proof was on the Abe government. She would not, in other words, willingly give up her exciting and well-paying job to retire to home life and start breeding for Japan.

There is the trust issue, to be sure, as the feeling that "Japan is past it" is going to be hard to dispel. A government as right-wing as that of Mr. Abe is going to leave the impression that it will do as little as possible to reverse the brewing Japanese catastrophe. This is also (no kidding!) unhelpful, as well. If we now return to France, we see that French women are quite confident that many family-friendly social programs are not going to be reversed anytime soon, and as such it is probably quite safe to conceive several children (France pays on a sliding scale, apparently).

So France will be around for a long time to come, whereas many other nations cannot even begin to say the same. "Aha!" you might say. What about the United States with its huge pending immigration bill? Can't nations import skilled workers en masse (to stick with French idioms) as required? Isn't that what the United States and Canada are doing right now, with all sorts of bonuses for people coming to Alberta?

No, this is a short-term solution for a long-term problem. Essentially beggaring thy neighbor cannot work because whatever you make with your new workers cannot readily be sold overseas. How can it, apart from niche markets here and there? If you purloin workers from overseas and hence weaken those economies, who is going to buy your nice shiny new cars and glitzy gimmicks?

At best, you will see your sales either stagnate or decline, and then what has been gained? However, the United States is going to go ahead with this plan and will gain a few years before hard-pressed CEOs go running to Washington looking for new handouts. I think the scorecard must read Socialism 1, Capitalism 0.

Okay, I can hear you ask, so what? So what if a bunch of undersexed Japanese men prefer to drink sake and watch scantily clad maidens in porn or anime movies as a proxy for the real thing? The trouble is that there are (in this wretched financial global economy) going to be a lot of knock-on effects.

If we take the example of Japanese government bonds (JGBs), what happens to the popular ten-year maturities if some learned papers are put out by Goldman Sachs or Bank of Tokyo decrying what is happening and wondering just how Japan will be able to finance or repay existing bonds as they become due? True, we are not going to see substantial reductions in the Japanese population overnight, but if potential investors are warned that within a generation there are going to be problems along these lines, then interest coupons on either existing or to-be-issued JGBs will be jacked up, possibly sharply, with the prospects of a severe recession—combined with a falling number of young people available to do jobs that will still need skilled workers.

This will ripple around the world, and it will not be rectified by a simple change of money supply issuance because there is a fundamental reason why this recession is happening. Yes, even America, with tens of millions of immigrants coming to its shores to fight fertility problems, may see a lack of jobs for all of these poor souls who may then simply turn tail and go home— probably to rapturous welcomes, given their highly in-demand skill sets.

Nevertheless, we are looking at a real recession problem not that many years down the road, and to reiterate, this will not be a recession caused by tangled money supplies and overvalued exchange rates—it will be a *real* recession caused by collapsing markets globally. Bonds have a tendency to discount this sort of bad news. I see nothing but bad news here, sad to say.

So let's sum up this probably overlong article. Japanese women seem to be most unwilling to perform the major function of women: to guarantee the continuance of Japanese society by having babies. If this refusal continues (and there is no indication that it will change), then Japan is finished as the nation we know today. Sorry, that's just the way it is.

Japanese women have apparently given up, caught between the cost of living, of housing in particular, and relationships that are not all that might be promised. They wonder why their country has not already collapsed, what with the probable lies surrounding Fukushima and who knows what else waiting in the wings.

In their hearts, they probably wonder why it is that their prime minister worships the past glories of the Japanese military and cannot see why he does not know what is changing so rapidly in his country. They probably even wonder if there will be a call for elder Japanese to be euthanized, and then what?

The Japanese seem to have a death wish in their popular culture as represented by anime. In three such movies I have seen, Japan is either wiped out completely (as in *Vexille*) or comes perilously close (in the Appleseed series). Even in the 1995 classic *Blue Seed*, Japan is on the verge of being turned into a nation of plants, only to be saved at the last minute. What is with all of this cultural flagellation, anyhow? If these films truly represent the inner feelings of Japan, then I cannot see any way for Japan to avoid completing its ritualistic suicide with women simply closing their wombs.

I should write a bit more on this, both on behalf of Japan and also South Korea. What do their women want? I do not believe that Japanese women want to even try to raise a family in an urban mess such as Tokyo, or Nagoya, or Osaka, or fill in the blank. They are basically, as I read what they are thinking and doing, considering themselves only as baby machines, with nothing for themselves. This would be carried on even to the extent of having a normal husband-and-wife relationship, with husbands having to spend more and more time away from their homes and families because of ever-increasing corporate demands on their time. Japanese women, apparently, have no desire to spend their lives in such a manner.

The current Japanese government is now completely the wrong thing at the wrong time. Abe's main wish is to throw women a bone (so to speak) in regard to having children so that he can resume what is going to be one of the most conservative Japanese administrations in quite some time. Let us see if what he wants makes sense in the current environment of falling numbers of workers to handle major goods-producing jobs.

He wants to revise the Japanese postwar constitution so that Japan can start to intervene overseas again. Yes, this is couched in the most harmless of terms, but it seems to me that the hand of Washington's State Department can be detected here. Washington (despite all sorts of noises about "pivoting to Asia") really wants to try to corner Russia and to thereby defang Iran, making what is left of the Middle East oil fields as safe for United States interests as can be.

This means that Washington needs a reliable ally in East Asia to keep watch on North Korea and, to a much lesser extent, on China itself. So Mr. Abe, with a looming demographics crisis of unimaginable proportions, seems willing to commit possibly large numbers of young Japanese men to this refurbished military. This is insane, and one wonders just what pressures he has been put under to do this. What is the quid pro quo?

In South Korea, this situation is even more desperate. The fertility rate there is down to about 1.3, but this is well up from the 0.98 we saw not that many years ago. By the way, the Koreans have congratulated themselves on this fairly rapid turnaround, but whatever they are saying publicly, they must still be having severe doubts internally in private conversations. They are nowhere close to break-even, shall we call it, and in the major newspapers they are only starting to come to grips with the underlying cause of the problem.

This revolves around, predictably enough after looking at Japan, problems with women finding suitable men and reasonably priced housing. Plus, in Korea, very high school fees make having even one child problematical. As is the case with Tokyo, the Korean capital of Seoul now is home to close to 20 percent of the entire South Korean population. In a country with only a small amount of land area, the Koreans have crammed into Seoul more than twenty-two million people, making it the third-largest city in the world.

How can one cope with a declining fertility rate when the overriding national objective of government is economic and financial growth? Do they not realize the danger they are in?

I believe they do, but they have no way to rectify this without what so many bureaucrats would call starting a national panic. What I suspect is going on is what Washington is probably angling for in the entire region: merging the two Koreas, as we have discussed previously. With North Korea effectively removed from many contentious issues, South Korea could also breathe easier knowing that North Korean men would find it quite easy to have families very probably started by some sort of relocation allowance funded by various South Korean reunification funds which are known to exist. Housing in South Korea would be incredibly luxurious by their standards. Again, we should refer back to the reunification of the two Germanys at the end of the 1980s and early 1990 to see what happened. A solidarity tax was passed in the old West Germany to fund a great deal of the individual expenses associated with the reunification, and there is no reason to suppose that this would not happen today half a world away in Korea.

It would all be very expensive, to be sure, but Washington gets what it wants (which, in the final analysis, is the most important aspect of all of this). And South Korea would get its desires met as well, in the form of bigger families and more working-age men suddenly coming into the Southern workforce. Bit of a tough blow for North Korea's Kim, though!

However, in my view, the reunification would be nothing more than a short-term palliative. When all is said and done, the problems of finding more and more workers to fill empty South Korean jobs and give enough slack in the overall economy for renewed growth would probably "be handled." However, without additional longer-term ways of getting Koreans to produce more babies to offset a huge die-off over the next few decades, it will all probably be for naught.

And what about the United States, Canada, and the EU countries? What do they do, as they have (except for France) the same problems as Asia? The culture is somewhat different here. Canada ran a series of ads on television last year saying that Canada needed a lot of foreign workers because it was losing something like one thousand skilled workers every day due to the baby boomers finally becoming old enough to retire.

Easy-to-obtain visas let a *lot* of foreign workers into the country, but the visas were not properly issued. Instead of having many skilled workers taking jobs where they were needed (i.e., in the tar sands), unscrupulous managers hired many workers to do the so-called menial, low-paying jobs, which clearly was not intended.

This is being rectified as I write these lines, and probably no long-term damage to the Canadian labor structure will have been done. What struck my eye was that the federal agencies in Ottawa were willing to act very quickly to counteract what was thought (and is, clearly) to be a serious loss of highly skilled workers. They did not react like their Japanese and Korean counterparts did and simply say, "We are going to have problems over the next forty to fifty years, so there is not much that can be done now." They assumed that there was an imminent crisis and reacted. The fact that they reacted without enough thought is a different matter entirely.

The United States is using a different approach altogether. What has been done in the past was to open the floodgates for "the world's poor and dispossessed" and to use the idea of a melting pot so that new immigrants, no matter where they came from, would be welcome and would combine their skills with existing Americans for the betterment of the country as a whole.

Today we see a huge immigration bill slowly wending its way through Congress, and I suspect that Congress will probably give US businesses all they could dream of: skilled workers who will work for subpar wages and increase corporate profits again and again. If this means that undereducated and unskilled US workers are effectively thrown on the scrapheap, so be it! The number of workers coming to America will be staggering.

Some estimates I have seen, when one takes into account the families of immigrants, could boost the US population by 100 percent over the next twenty to thirty years, from 320 million to nearly two-thirds of a billion! That's a lot of people by any stretch, and I wonder where they will all go and what sorts of resources they will consume as they start their version of the American Dream.

In looking at the United States, we should consider also what leading political figures are doing about all of this and how it is likely to play out as time progresses. From what I have been able to find out, it seems that the US fertility rate among the white population is something like 1.5 or so. Adding in the very prolific Mexicans, it jumps up to perhaps 1.80 or 1.90, or not that far short of break-even at 2.1.

What is Hillary Clinton doing about all of this, and what does she probably feel about the whole thing? To answer this reasonably, I go back to the speech she gave in Los Angeles in November 2013, which was given to an overflow crowd of Spanish-speaking Los Angeles residents. Put simply, Latinos love her and will deliver their votes to her in overwhelming numbers.

If Hillary can get through Congress the immigration bill that has been talked about endlessly in the US press (and my bet is that she will, given the monumental short-sightedness of US businesses), then we shall see immense numbers of Mexicans come north.

Why is this? Hillary said that NAFTA (the free trade agreement binding Canada, the United States, and Mexico into an economic grouping) should be expanded through closer and closer relationships between the three NAFTA nations. It is clear, and I shall bet that the Republican leadership in Congress knows this better than anyone, that she wants to open the doors to skilled Mexican workers to come north.

Already we are seeing that deportation of Mexicans without the proper visas is diminishing. Mexicans who should be on their way back home are staying, in other words. If they stay and are legalized, with many of their friends and family invited to come to the United States, they will thank Hillary at the ballot box in 2016. The sheer numbers here may very well get an overwhelming majority to swing the election decisively to Hillary. Well, doesn't the GOP know this? Why are they trying to get the immigration bill passed?

This party is trapped by the desires of their supposed base—big business—to get cheap workers into the United States *now* so that wage bills can be cut back as soon as possible and profits can resume an uninterrupted flow upward. The big thing here is that new workers may not know much about what are called "fringe benefits" in the United States, and with health-care costs exploding, the costs to the big corporations are becoming most uncomfortable.

So, for them, do we see lower wages and fewer fringe benefits? What's not to like? So Speaker Boehner and the rest of the GOP bigwigs are caught trying to play politics while they are going to get trampled by Mexican workers coming north to vote for Hillary because she is perceived to be friendly to the aspirations of Mexican workers. What's a poor Republican to do? Nothing is the clear answer, except watch the future of your party simply disappear. (Perhaps this is another reason to get Texas Senator Ted Cruz on the ballot come November 2016, despite the clear handicap of his being born in Canada—a Constitutional no-no, or at least it is supposed to be.)

Finally, on this question of population and a lack of skilled workers, what can we learn from the EU, excluding France? In reading about the troubles in Germany (and this country, built on exports after WWII), one wonders if the Europeans have any clue. In Germany, the noted newspaper

Der Spiegel ran a couple of articles a year or so ago on a growing shortage of workers in southern Germany.

It seems that firms there, in the German industrial heartland, are short of something like five million workers but do not like the idea of filling out a massive number of government forms to get the required workers onboard. There is also the question of having to train the new workers to speak German, which apparently is time-consuming (read: expensive—can't have that, now can we?). All of which makes no sense. Why is this?

Well, Germany is part of the EU and hence can import workers from all over Europe as required, whether they speak German or not. In fact, there are German classes for new arrivals on an ongoing basis. What all this tells me is that there is an unhealthy streak of xenophobia in Germany, even to this day.

And what about places such as Italy, Spain, and Portugal, which also use the euro? How are they doing, and what is their outlook? Basically they vary between terrible and ghastly. Define those terms as you will; they are both Bad with a capital B. In Italy, we see persistent high unemployment, and the employment system, which has served Italy so well since the end of WWII, seems to be under threat.

This system revolved around the concept of a guaranteed job, which might sound "socialistic" to an American but worked very well over there. Now some of the high-brow EU leaders think that youngsters should quit these jobs and "see what you can find and what you can make of yourselves." Really? With very high unemployment, people are going to start quitting their jobs? All this so Italian companies can shed excess labor to be "more competitive."

The divide between management and shop-floor people is as wide as ever, and this is with the population problems Italy currently suffers under. The fertility rate there is far below the critical 2.1 level. Population has been falling for some years now, to boot. The country never seemed to be able to adjust to the single-currency euro, as the government in Rome had always devalued the old lira whenever things "needed to get done."

This is no longer possible, for obvious reasons, and it does not look like the economy is going to recover to any great extent when Germany is doing moderately well. There has generally been a divide between northern and southern Europe for decades, if not centuries, and there is no indication that this will become any better.

In fact, with Germany needing skilled workers and the US immigration system looking to vacuum up just about anything that moves in the next decade or so, how can things get better for Italy and southern Europe in general? It can't, is probably the most reasonable answer.

Elsewhere in what is fashionable (but, of course, politically incorrect) to call the backward parts of the EU, we see Spain and Portugal. Both countries adopted the euro thinking that it would be so good for their economies to have a bit of internal German-style discipline, but this has not been the case. Spain has seen sky-high unemployment at something like 27 percent, with youth jobless at perhaps twice this level. Just imagine what the headlines would be if we saw numbers like this in the United States.

So far, the Spaniards have suffered in silence, and I suspect that many of the brighter and more skilled workers will be making tracks for the United States after the immigration bill there becomes law. Why not? Given the huge numbers of Mexicans already in the United States, with many more to come (Hillary pushing the gates open herself), there would not be a language barrier to any great extent.

Additionally, with many nations in Central and South America having Spanish as a first language (who says colonial rule doesn't have long-term benefits?), there is plenty of opportunity elsewhere. Spain is not going to have an easy time, it seems to me. Again, for your own contemplation, with a fertility rate of 1.5, how *can* Spain recuperate?

Lastly, we look at little Portugal. Why bother with this minor flyspeck on the EU scene, you may ask? Well, the leader of the EU comes from there, and it is another example of a country at the periphery of this vast trading bloc being left to twist in the wind. (One wonders what the Ukraine and the other Eastern European nations are going to do, over time, when they all subject to the EU monetary prison which is the euro!)

And what does poor little Portugal (which has been desperately poor for so much of its history) do to try and alleviate unemployment, which is not as bad as Spain's but bad enough? Again, we go to its history and see that there were nations in Africa that were colonized by Portugal in the frenzy by Europe, in days gone by, to grab what others possessed, come what may.

I look at the country of Angola, which is Portuguese-speaking and immensely rich because of its oil deposits. True, it is ruled by what many regard to be a despotic form of government, but no one wants to rock a very rich boat. Portuguese citizens go there and set up shop with all sorts of ideas, a lot of them in the electronic communications industry. It is not hard to get a visa to go there for many years and make money. Clearly this cannot be done back home in Portugal in the present state of circumstances.

In a study done by *der Spiegel* last year, we saw that the Angolan economy from 2000 to 2013 grew a total of more than 230 percent. I would imagine that the rulers of that nation cannot be displeased at what they are seeing, although the gap between the newly rich and rural poverty is immense. Nevertheless, how can any nation—especially one like Portugal—allow entrepreneurial types to simply leave, taking their money and skills with them? How can Portugal, with a fertility rate of 1.5, do this for any decent period of time and apparently not realize the danger they are putting themselves in?

Well, let's wrap up this section on population, shall we? How is it that global population experts can say (apparently endlessly) that the world is overpopulated, and yet I can write for as long as I have on the serious problems faced by the so-called advanced nations and their population imbalances?

How, you may well ask, can we reconcile these seemingly disparate viewpoints? What follows is politically incorrect, but I have to write it. If we take a country like Niger (an impoverished wreck of a nation in Central Africa), we see the fertility rate at something over 7. Yes, I would imagine that many of these children perish in infancy, given the primitive conditions into which they are born, but this is the sort of place where much of the world's population comes into existence.

In a much larger nation population-wise, such as Nigeria, we see this key measurement at 5.3. It is estimated, as the relatively pampered population of the West sees a continuous decline over the next half century or so, that we could see maybe half a billion Nigerians—all things being equal.

This is the crux of the problem. Vast numbers of human beings are classified as "useless" because they have no skills that are recognized as being worth anything in terms of the economy-driven West. Effectively, the feeling is, what good are people who spend short lives grubbing around in the dirt and have no idea what a computer hard drive is?

What good is an illiterate African (or Indian from one of the lower castes) as someone who cannot build a house or dissect a balance sheet? Why do countries such as Italy stop hoards of luckless would-be immigrants from Africa from coming there, even though the Italian population situation is such that additional people to do various menial jobs should be in demand?

One of the great sentiments from the US Revolutionary War period (and perhaps one of the most profound ever) was that all men are created equal. Until very recently, it was the shining light in US society and certainly was the guiding force for the US Civil Rights era. In today's world, with its unremitting focus on money, power, and a clearly unsupportable idea that economic growth can be unstoppable, this idea of the ages is sadly no more.

Looking at Germany with its latent xenophobia, and Italy (even though it needs the people) turning away African economic immigrants by the boatload, I wonder what these nations are thinking as a collective. With a falling population (in the case of Italy) and a weak fertility rate, do they really want to cease to exist as a viable nation a generation or so down the road?

Why do they bury their heads on this? Well, I'm sure we know the answer: no black Africans allowed here, as they are inferior. There! I have said it, and I challenge you to prove me wrong. In the case of Japan (to take one final example), public opinion polls say, by a large margin, that the Japanese do *not* want large-scale immigration at all. Bye-bye, Japan. Do the math.

In all this intellectual tussle, we keep coming back to President H. Clinton and her open-door policy to fellow NAFTA member, Mexico. It will happen if she wins; bank on it! The United States will scour the globe looking for potential immigrants to come to the land of the free.

In some articles I have read, these would-be immigrants do not even have to bring their skills, if they have any. The immigration bill, in one of its editions, allows for something that the United States has not encouraged for many decades now: unskilled immigrants. What a damning blow to the tens of millions of Americans who do not have a job or who do not have elementary skills to even seek one! Yet, if the United States starts to hoover up all of the reasonable-looking immigrants, what happens to Japan, Italy, Germany, Portugal, Spain, and the rest?

There will be two classes of people in the world: those who have skills and can go anywhere, and those who have little to offer and will be left alone to breed and consume. Until the baby boomers start to die off in large numbers (which, obviously, must happen), global population will continue to grow.

All men will continue not to be created equal! The remarkable thing about this horrible attitude is that it is so wrong. Old stereotypes die so hard, it seems. Consider modern Africa, if you would. *Der Spiegel* (yes, I do read other newspapers, but this one always seems to have cutting-edge analysis) did a piece on Africa recently.

Far from being a continent full of headhunters and disease, with possibly prehistoric animals in its trackless swamps, in many countries (thirteen I count) there are more cell phone contracts per hundred people than there are in the United States. A good comment I read dealt with an entrepreneur who had set up his own company and was working on a way to bring cell technology to really back-of-beyond villages. These villagers would then use their cell phones to do rudimentary banking!

This is amazing, and one wonders about countries such as Italy, which seemingly have no interest in "backward Africans." Their country is slowly falling apart (population and fertility rate-wise), and they turn their backs on geniuses such as these? Perhaps there is a turning point in European history where European states fade into history, and we might be living in it now. Perhaps I shouldn't pick on Italy, as I am sure that many other European nations are probably seeing the same sort of attitude in their domestic populations. Fine, they shall all share the same fate.

Well, I have written my piece on population problems and how they are likely to be resolved. This always assumes that there is not some bloody, God-awful war that eats up millions of young lives. Women will be included this time as well, sadly, which will exacerbate the shortage of what we might call "fertility rate workers" even more. (This question just occurred to me: Does the United States want the unskilled workers in the immigration bill to be able to join the military and so preserve the precious skilled workers?)

However, for Americans as a whole (and this is especially true with the enormous quantities of baby boomers either retired or about to be retired), what happens to their pensions? What happens with Social Security, which supposedly has the vast resources to pay the boomers off for many years, given longevity rates these days? Can it survive with perhaps two or three workers to pay the benefits of one retiree?

And this subject must go hand-in-glove with the analysis of badly skewed populations in much of the world—as we have just discussed. Tens of millions of baby boomers are going to retire and want pensions, ideally commensurate with the salaries they received just before they retired. This cannot possibly happen, as we shall now see in the last chapter of this book. It will not be pleasant reading, but for those who have stuck with me for all of this time, I urge you in no uncertain terms to read on.

CHAPTER 4

Pensions—What a Mess! No Round-
the-World Trips for You in Your
Golden Years, Sorry to Say

Many years ago, when I was much younger, I can recall learned debates on this subject, with many people saying that without at least ten workers to support one retiree, the system could not possibly work. Lots of press was devoted to this, and because (in my opinion) it dealt with a problem many years down the road, no one in Congress really cared. No tough decisions were made, and we were just left to muddle through. Even the retirement age was not raised, which I would have thought was quite obvious.

Can't raise retirement ages, now can we? It might lead to votes being lost for the Congressman who proposed this sort of thing, much less voted for it! It was said that Social Security was the third rail of politics: touch it and you die.

So, with the backbone of marshmallows, Congress did the absolute minimum, and look where we are now.

All we have is that "Social Security will be there when you need it" and no math to back up what is probably an absurd claim. Unless ... unless. Could it be that some far-sighted people in Congress (there are bound to be one or two in that lot) have run some numbers and feel that with the arrival of scores of millions of immigrants, the FICA taxes will take care of the immediate problem?

Maybe this is so, but what happens when this set of immigrants retire "some years down the road"? What happens to that crisis? Ah, fugetaboutit! That's then, and not my problem. Once a marshmallow, always a marshmallow. However, in the overall pension scheme, Social Security is just one piece of the puzzle. What else is there to worry about? Plenty!

What happens with corporate and state/municipal pensions? What happens if you are about to be paid by Detroit, or a Detroit wannabe? What happens to private 401(k) plans (RRSP in Canada) that a person might have been contributing into all of their working lives? How will these fare if other plans are struggling to stay afloat?

When Detroit was sharing the spotlight of shame, I read that some public servants there who had worked for thirty years or so and were counting on a decent pension from the city were going to be sorely disappointed. In one case, someone who was counting on perhaps a $3,000 per month pension wound up looking at getting maybe sixteen cents on the dollar—say $500 per month if he was lucky. It seems that the finances in that wretched city are tangled and corrupt beyond measure.

Unions screaming for "more, more, ever more" and corruption on an apparently epic scale have decimated pension reserves until they are worth very little at all. Pensioners in that luckless city are to be paid in promises, it seems. These were so eagerly believed in, and life went on with promises as effective currency until it all came tumbling down, as it ultimately had to.

Am I being unduly harsh on what was once the Motor City? No, there are others in a mess, but none on the scale of Detroit. However, what about the next step up: the individual states? There are two I have been watching, and while they are not in the news at this time on this subject, the problems they face have not gone away.

These are California (upon which the economic fate of the United States probably depends, given its enormous size, economic depth, and diversity) and Illinois. I do not think it is much of an exaggeration to say that the health of this latter state rests upon the City of Broad Shoulders, which is, of course, Chicago. Unfortunately, as is with the case of nearby Michigan, too much of this state rests on the health of one city (Michigan rising or falling, mostly falling, with Detroit)—and this is Chicago.

The unions and a series of city administrations have done the pension system there no good at all, and some of the pension funds there are only about 40 to 50 percent funded. What does this mean? It means that out of every dollar in pension payment liabilities, the paying authority has between 40 and 50 cents in assets. Normally, when a pension falls to as low as 80 cents on the dollar, it is time for remedial action, so you only guess how pension managers there must be tearing their hair out these days.

In my experience, a well-run pension fund has one hundred cents on the dollar (or more) to match liabilities. In reading up on all of this, I am astounded that Chicago seems to have no real concerns at its appalling level of funding, and I wait for the day when the headlines blare that "Chicago pensioners will have to take a 'haircut' (discount) because of the poor state of the books."

I can't see how this can be avoided, and I pity the poor pensioners who will wake up one morning to a letter that starts, "Dear Sir/Madam, we regret to inform you that due to problems beyond our control, we are cutting the amount of your monthly pension check to $1,500 from $3,000." It is coming; bet on it. A case of corruption run amok, I would say.

California (I hadn't forgotten them either) has done unbelievably stupid things with its pension liabilities, and as is the case with so many other entities around, the United States seems to have regarded the pot of money put aside as some sort of slush fund to be used when it is politically necessary.

Pensions need a lot of time to grow their assets to make their payments. They also require an annual average return of about 8 percent to make these payments work mathematically at the end (i.e., what you get in your final payment when you turn sixty or sixty-five or whatever). What many people do not realize is that it is the compounding effect of all of these returns that really juices up the payouts.

By the way, while I think about it, you may have read about funding many decimated pension plans (and this may ultimately include Social Security) by hiking the monthly premiums on your paycheck. This means, in plain English, your deductions are going to go quite a bit higher. We should also note that this concept of compounding is going to make itself felt here as well.

If you are only a few years from retirement, then maybe you will not be hit on your pay as much as someone who is twenty-five, let us say. Why is this? If you are twenty-five, then your contributions have a full forty years to compound. If you are sixty, then the compounding factor is effectively irrelevant. Your pension fund will go (as everybody else does!) where the money is—and, needless to say, how it is generated.

For example, if we look at a return of 8 percent per annum (simple interest) on your contribution of $100 after thirty years, we would see it worth $340. If we compound this 8 percent at 8 percent (that is to say, your return of 8 percent is in turn reinvested at 8 percent for each and every year you contribute) we get something quite different. Then your $100 would be worth $1,000 (ten times as much, versus just $340), and that makes the entire system work. If we remove some of the compounding for whatever reason (i.e., corruption or whatever) then the returns take quite a hit. To boil this paragraph down, I have seen some cities in California showing a return of just 1.5 percent. This is bad, *bad* news if you are retiring a few years from now.

Am I intending to frighten you? Yes, quite frankly, I am! No, I do not take some sort of sadistic pleasure in doing this, but it is mandatory in the remaining years before the pension math collides with reality that I tell all and sundry about my fears. No matter what you hear from embarrassed and embattled pension boards, just keep in mind that large amounts of cash are required to pay pensioners (baby boomers) month in and month out. Keep in mind also that increased payouts will be required as inflation protection riders kick in—and kick in without limit as time goes by. So what? you may say.

You could claim that this is allowed for in the calculations when the pensions were set up, and you would be right—up to a point. However, if more and more cash has to be paid out, then either more cash has to be taken in from pension dues when the baby boomers were working (and now their successors), or there has to be a better return for the fund.

Now if pension funds have an interruption in their flow on money for some years (as has happened under the very easy money policy by the fed for a lengthy period of time now), where is this extra money going to come from, especially if pensions exist on the magic of compound interest? With inflation riders, the squeeze on returns even at 8 percent is probably close to absolute, and any breakdown in these forms of income will simply not be available to be made up.

What about individual pension plans—the so-called 401(k) plans? Aren't these going to save the day—those people who could afford to put money aside to fund them in an age of squeezed paychecks and the like? I do not believe so. In assessing a study of how people manage money on the Chicago Board of Trade, we see some truly dismal numbers. Some years back it was claimed that out of every twenty traders, fully nineteen of them (that is 95 percent) lose money.

A more recent study shows that traders are doing a bit better with "just" seventeen out of twenty losing money—or 85 percent. This means that nearly all people who trade to try and boost the derisory returns available from the interest rate markets are simply not making it, shall we say. When one adds in the fees taken by the trustees who hold the monies or invest on behalf on individuals, the overall success rate is quite dismal. Clearly, and this is another way of putting it, if society was expecting people to be able to provide for themselves in their old age, that is not going to be the case.

So to avoid all of the problems associated with a lack of pension income for the elderly starting literally anytime going forward, something will have to be done. However, it seems to me that while there were as many trillions as needed to bail out the US banking system after its absurd attempt to make dud mortgages sound (the terrible mortgage crisis starting in late 2007, which nearly toppled every other banking system across the globe), none will be made available to assist pensions.

It would be held (and this would definitely be true if a right-wing Republican wins the White House in 2016) that this something would be "socialist intervention" in a free-market economy, which is something the average American does not stand for. Okay, so maybe I am being a little harsh here with my criticism, but there is an underlying point to all of this: Where is the money coming from to do all of the bailing?

We hear today deafening cries that President Obama is bankrupting America for generations to come with his free-spending ways, and these know-it-all critics point to the staggering (at present writing) accumulated federal deficit of $17.5 trillion.

This is very unfair because without congressional consent, the US president cannot spend a dime of taxpayer money. However, it is the perception that matters. No matter who wins in 2016, and I am of the firm belief that it will be Mrs. Clinton, the cries about the pension deficit will be unending.

Yes, I know what I have written about the likely GOP response to this mess, but something will have to be done whether the GOP likes it or not. The difference will be one of degree. Where is a large enough clump of money, anywhere, to accomplish all of this pension reform? Some of the right-wing blogs have been floating a trial balloon that *all* pensions will have to be nationalized and most likely merged with Social Security.

You would then get one monthly check from the SS Administration instead of one from them, one from your former employer or employers, and whatever you can scrounge from your own 401(k). This will be very bad news for the few who have been able, one way or another, to provide for themselves and their families, and perhaps these few should have a long think as to what to do with their (so far) profitable portfolios. Perhaps cashing out a sizeable portion of it and buying gold? I am, of course, guessing, and I would imagine that older and wiser heads than mine have considered this and many other possibilities.

Many years ago, I read that perhaps two-thirds of retired Americans (back then) only had their monthly SS check as their sole income. They lived in desperate poverty and were, literally, one illness away from being completely bankrupted.

What a harrowing way to live! Of the remaining 33 percent of retired Americans, perhaps 25 percent were just getting by with a small degree of comfort with SS checks and whatever else they were lucky enough to be able to acquire during their working lives. Only the remaining 10 percent (or fewer) were able to live their retirements as they may have imagined throughout their lives.

This was quite pathetic, and I wondered just how these poor souls had been so badly misled with their pension funds. Surely, something would be done? Well, a few years ago I revisited the problem and found to my amazement that two-thirds of Americans still had only SS to tide them over. There were a couple of percentage points' difference in the other two categories, but that was it.

Why do I point this out? I merely want to say that the endless barrage of "buy that new car or new house—you owe it to yourself," which the average free-spending American is subject to through his or her working life, has been responsible for what we are witnessing today.

The "good life" has conquered all rational views of how life should be lived, and it therefore stands to reason that the response to the now unstoppable pension crisis (and that word is not misused, sorry to say) will be handled in a similar fashion: don't worry, good times will still roll.

This is, of course, quite impossible looking at the numbers, so what *is* to be done? As the title of this book asks, what *is* happening? Don't worry your sweet little heads about it! Uncle Sam will take care of it, as he has taken care of just about everything so far. The bottom line will be that SS will bail out everybody and everything, to an extent, and that everybody will have—as the end result—some sort of monthly living stipend.

There will be all sorts of conditions laid out, all of which will be said to "ensure the solvency of Social Security virtually indefinitely." The age of eligibility for SS will be raised, possibly at one step, from sixty-two to sixty-six, and then to seventy to cut down on the number of early retirees that the math underlying SS simply cannot support.

There will be (because of the vast number of Americans who have nothing but SS when they retire) a conversion of SS to some sort of "means-tested" program, which, in simple terms, says that if you are making more than $50,000 when you retire then you do not need the basic SS payment; you will have to get by on your own resources and company pension plans (this is the part which has been absorbed into SS as noted above). It will not be pretty, unless you are very poor and are now feeling better that so many others have been dragged down to your level.

The other possibility is something that I am seeing in South Korea. There is more to this Asian powerhouse than opposition to North Korea and the making of Hyundai cars. A series of articles in the newspaper *Chosen Ilbo* on June 9, 2014, talks about the plight of Koreans under their version of Social Security.

Because it is a weak system (how else do you think that the funding of the Korean economic miracle after the devastating war from 1950 to 1953 was obtained?) these Koreans will probably have to work until they are seventy-one years old or so. Forty percent of the retiring baby boomers are going to be living in penury in retirement. Fifty percent need a stipend from their children to make ends meet, which makes one wonder how these children are going to be able to fund having families of their own and hence overcome the fertility rate problem for their country (knee bone connected to the thighbone).

Finally, many Koreans associate retirement with loneliness and poverty in any event. It is a ghastly scenario and one that, I am afraid to say, awaits so many elderly Americans who were told that the system will make them secure in their retirement and that "Social Security will be there when you need it." Well, I suppose that it is, to some extent, but it seems a fair bet that it is not what many Americans had envisioned for themselves in their Golden Years.

Let's finish off this segment of the book by looking at what I had to write about retirement in the newsletter. Yes, there will be some duplication of material from what has gone before, but I want you to see how it all continues to fall together:

> There has been a fair bit of commentary recently on this subject in the blogs and also "regular" channels. Being an elderly gentleman myself and a fully fledged pensioner, it behooves me to at least have a look at all of this. I have had several letters from some readers (thank you, DK—and others) who do not wish to accept all of the bad news that I so routinely pour out in these newsletters.
>
> Well, I am sorry about all of this apparent negativity, but I have to call things in the way that forty-six years of training has taught me! The overall situation is unremitting grim as we look forward immediately into 2014, and then into the problems of the 2015–2020 period. Debt is the main killer here on many fronts, from overstretched consumers who simply cannot say a simple no to the latest bit of hi-tech glitter, to

governments who are generally overindebted—badly so in many cases.

Whether it is a consumer who simply says, "I gotta have this gizmo—it is sooo me" or a government that never met a war or security issue it didn't like, debt is debt, and it is an immense killer of citizens and nations.

Why do I bring this up when it comes to the subject of pensions and the like? Well, pension funds have to invest large amounts of money for their clients, and the huge debt issues running roughshod through the global economies are causing all sorts of grave distortions.

For example, in the early part of this century, home loans (mortgages) have been forced to become more borrower-friendly so as to keep what was an overpriced housing market from falling apart. The net result of all of this was the fiasco in 2007–08, which nearly resulted in a complete collapse of banking systems everywhere. As of today, it is my understanding that banks are still in a dreadful to-do on their balance sheets from this mortgage mess and are speculating in various financial markets in what may be termed close to insanity regarding positioning.

I, of course, refer you back to "God" and his immense oil positions noted for some time now. Into these various messes comes the poor pension manager. With long-term interest rates now at only something slightly shy of 4 percent, other things have to be tried.

Why is this? I was shown some interesting figures recently that clearly demonstrated just how stressed pension funds really are. We are looking at a minimum of an 8 percent return on assets to be able to meet the future demands of pensioners. Now it is clear that 4 percent Treasury returns (at best) will not be able to cover an 8 percent call on assets. What I had failed to consider adequately was the compounding effects of liabilities versus these assets.

The study I saw used a figure of 9 percent for liabilities, and I suppose that is reasonable, but what I failed to look at properly was the compounding effect of all of this. Simply put, if assets are to cover liabilities, then the assets must grow at the same rate as pension liabilities. The trouble (as any pension manager will tell you) is that whatever happens, the liabilities are going to grow and grow. This negative growth (overall pension fund health, essentially) will be there whatever happens to the asset side of your pension's balance sheet.

If we have a problem with interest rate receipts from a failing bond market (this is, of course, in terms of interest payable to the pension fund), then a gap will quickly emerge and will, unless checked, simply get larger and larger. Ah, the magic of compound growth on the wrong side of the ledger!

So what is a fund manager to do? What is he or she allowed to do under law? Does a certain amount of the pension's assets have to be invested in US Treasuries? Can so-called speculative trades be allowed? The king of all of these bond pensions is the mainstay of the US system, and that is Social Security. This has to be invested in US Treasury bonds and so, these days, SS is suffering with interest rate yields on its portfolio probably not keeping pace with the burgeoning baby boomer retirees.

Yes, this sort of demographic bulge can be allowed for in initial calculations, but if anything goes wrong with (let us say) Congress raiding what must be a very tempting financial pot, then how is it to be made up? It is a long way from my parents paying in something like $3.00 a month to fund their retirement, to the maximum annual contribution of $7,049.40 today. Is this sort of markup reflecting what has been added to and reassigned by Congress to the SS system over the decades?

What else can be given to fund SS as the overall economic situation (as measured by the yearly deficit) forces Congress to look for large quantities of money that have not yet been assessed for tax revenue purposes? The main problem here for SS, given its exposure to bonds, must be if the new Fed Chairman, Janet Yellen, allows interest rates to drift down to a negative level.

What happens to a bond portfolio if, instead of receiving interest from the federal government, it has to pay for the privilege of holding US financial paper? (In other words, interest rates become negative.) If SS has to pay out to retirees and also to the federal treasury, then it will soon have to dip into its overall assets/reserves to continue to make all of the required payments. Again, with this sort of major upset of baby boomer retirement payments, we are going to see significant problems come forward for Congress to address once again.

It will not be pleasant to watch (or to fund, come to think of it) what is done to rectify these problems, and my personal belief is that the conservatives in those august bodies may simply allow SS to roll over and die in what they believe is a long overdue death.

There appear to be many such legislators who simply do not believe that SS was ever meant to be, or is at best some giant and unaffordable Ponzi scheme. In reality, it is what so many other pension funds are: a way for the elderly to live with a modicum of dignity in their declining years.

If it is not to be abolished in some manner, then (and this is my favorite, given the incredible money problems the United States suffers from) it will be sold off and privatized, with all that this may imply for Grandpa and Grandma's monthly benefit checks. (Hint: in this case, think of great volatility in monthly payouts, as the acquiring banks will want to grind the funds they are acquiring to generate some good trading profits. Granny and Gramps will probably not participate, benefit-wise, in this trading orgy to any great extent.)

I have heard from some of my readers that it is impossible to sell off SS to banks or to anybody else. Why, these people ask, would anybody want to buy up a bankrupt fund that is composed of government bonds, which are on the verge of suffering a great calamity within two years? The clear implication is that such paper (full faith and credit) is effectively worthless, and who on earth would buy paper that is either value-impaired now or will be in just a few short years?

With all liabilities and no assets, SS will be exposed for what so many conservative Congressmen believe: a worthless Ponzi scheme. I disagree, provided that the sale of SS takes place when the value of US Treasuries is still unquestioned by the markets as a whole. This would have to be fairly soon, if it is going to happen at all.

If the fed will act as a buyer of last resort for this paper, then cash can still be obtained from such a sale. Let us see how all of this plays out. SS is in a mess to be sure, but if the US dollar holds up on global exchange markets, then perhaps more time can be gained. Don't get ahead of yourself, in other words.

I write about SS in some depth, as it is probably the bluest of the blue chip funds. What about others, which would include other state and local pensions and so on down to corporate and then individual funds? The article I have been referring to (by Ben Inker of the firm GMO) has assessed this in depth.

The big thing that stuck me so forcefully is what this compounding can really do. There is an excellent chart in the analysis that I am not able to reproduce here, which shows that by next year (i.e., not some far-off date that means little to most people), US public pension funds will be showing an asset/liability gap of something like $1.2 trillion. How is this to be made up? Can it be funded at all? The asset/liability mismatch was well managed until the mortgage debacle in 2007–08, when desperately needed capital gains from equities simply were not there because equities completely fell apart. Mortgage debacles will do that to a pension fund.

In assessing all of the foregoing, before I wrote this piece and saw Inker's exceptional analysis, I believed that the current great run-up in stocks would have covered whatever temporary shortfall may have occurred back then. This seems not to be the case. Allowing for this damnable liability compounding and, very probably, some drawdown of the asset base to pay "temporary benefits" to retirees, market losses (more accurately "lack of gains") have not yet been redeemed from current price improvements.

This is another way of writing what I have been saying in the last few sentences. In turn, this can only imply, with the derisory returns from bonds, that public pension funds are in a dreadful mess. To underline this, we can only recall that the city of Detroit seems to have been rather creative with its accounting assumptions for its public pensions, from what I have read in some area newspapers. And now, with various claims against the fund and the city, it may be able to pay out only sixteen cents on the dollar to needy pensioners.

These poor folk seem to have been betrayed, sacrificed on the altars of political expediency during their working lives. The promise that "it will be there when you need it" has proven to be so similar to other such promises: hollow when monetary push comes to payment shove.

Well, this sounds like rather high and grandiose verbiage, so where is the one thing I always look for, which is "follow the money"? Yes, it is here as well. We need look no further than Mr. Ben Bernanke and the Federal Reserve.

For some time now, this once symbol of financial probity has been ladling out the sum of $85 billion a month to its member banks by buying US Treasuries (and some mortgages) and printing the money to pay for them. The banks have been the big beneficiaries here, as their ruined balance sheets from the 2007–08 mortgage mess remain in grave condition. These institutions, from what I can determine, have been using this money to make money by speculating to a fare-thee-well in just about anything that trades.

Any and all derivatives are fair game here, and I wonder what the average citizen would think if he or she knew that with this printed money the banks would be trading in such instruments as option spreads on interest rate barbells? (Don't ask!)

However, it is the stock market that interests me here. All day and every day, I seem to be reading all about how the Dow is grossly overpriced by all objective measures and why it is due for a crash of historic proportions. However, this is not the case to date. If one follows the flow of funds, one sees that equities are strongly bullish and likely to remain that way. Money is pouring into equity funds of all descriptions, and the Dow is strongly bid, to put it mildly! The target here is Dow 19,000.

Yes, I am aware that in 2014 we shall probably have a medium-sized war somewhere or other, and wars are not good for equities. However, this would be the correction that so many people are awaiting, in my view. If we have a moderately quick conflict and then the bond crisis in 2015, equities may move sharply higher—all to the benefit of badly damaged pension funds.

It is the belief of many analysts that Mr. Bernanke's largesse in buying bonds (QE or $85 billion a month) was really designed to increase the value of equities to try to bail out desperately flailing pension funds. I would agree with this, although because of the misery of stock losses in 2007–08 and the inexorable grinding of compound liabilities, I do not think it will be even close to being enough assistance and will only gain a bit of time until something more dramatic will have to happen.

However, as we have been wondering in previous newsletters, it is more likely that Fed leader Janet Yellen is going to wind up doing the reverse. Oh, granted, she will try to crank up the economy with more of the Bernanke ultraeasy money policy, but that is having a terrible effect on bondholders. Interest rates yielding less than 4 percent are useless for long-term capital appreciation, as we have been discussing.

The real problem for pension funds must therefore be what happens if she lets interest rates fall to negative levels (see above). People will be seeing the value of their bank accounts fall, possibly dramatically, depending on just how far Yellen lets rates fall.

In this environment, equities will do well. Think about this. If you have a choice between paying a bank 1 to 2 percent a year to watch your checking account, or investing in a name company that pays a dividend of 3 percent or more, what are you going to do?

It is fairly obvious, I would have thought, especially if you are a long-term holder of a pension fund. True, it is not enough to offset the accrued liabilities, which are compounding (back to that again), and this will still probably ultimately sink pension funds—purely on a cash flow basis.

However, if the Dow runs to 31,000 (as I saw in an ultrabullish ad today), then maybe you are still all right. However, if you *need* the Dow to run to 31,000 (possibly higher with some Dow components) then you really have to back to the edge of a cliff to do your fighting. It is all so very dangerous, no matter what the US authorities try.

The damage to the real economy done by ultralow interest rates to date (and heading lower if my prognosis is correct) has been to twist it and stretch it in unnatural ways, to the detriment of all.

One thing I should mention here is what may happen if pension funds start to go down in large numbers with several million old-age citizens are not able to collect enough to live on and, consequently, are reduced to penury. My sense is that something will have to be done about this, given what may be a very real fear by the central authorities of mounting disquiet in the citizenry as things go from bad to worse.

We have had a look-see at what SS and (in all probability) state and local pension funds are going to be going through. The money will not be there in anything like what has been promised, as the accruals simply do not make the sense required to do this. So when many other US cities (and states like Illinois and possibly

California) start to use what will probably be called the Detroit Formula by going through bankruptcy as a means of getting their books in order, what will be done?

One cannot have scores of towns and cities simply deciding that pensioners will get it in the neck at sixteen cents on the dollar because the banks or other preferred creditors are demanding (and receiving through a compliant court system) their pound of flesh.

The outcry will be deafening, and even hard-core GOP members of Congress, who may entertain severe doubts about the whole idea of public pensions (i.e., SS, as noted above), will not be able to resist doing something. What will probably happen is that the bankrupt pension funds will probably be folded into SS in some manner.

This would be doubly attractive if the banks are in the process of taking over SS. As this would represent a possibly serious cost to the taxpayer, we shall be told that "those responsible will be brought to justice" and the American version of very public show trials will be witnessed by all and sundry. Justice must at least be *seen* to work.

As regards corporate pension plans, I have had two instances of firsthand experience as to how corporations will use just about any trick to try to bring back onto the corporate balance sheet what are deemed "excess returns" that the pension manager happens to make in a given year.

I would have considered that this was a very good way to see corporate pension funds to be something less than what may have been promised (either explicitly or implied) to a soon-to-be pensioner. If there are a lot of pensioners in this position, what are we to make of corporate pension funds? Will they be treated in a similar fashion to failing state pensions? My guess is that they will be, simply because who is going to differentiate between poor pensioners under the state or company system?

Lastly, what about private pensions—the legendary 401(k) that has been around for so long? Here it may be a little bit different. There may be quite a few plans that have done what they were supposed to. They, the plan holders, will have worked diligently to provide for themselves and their families. Yes, there will be some plan holders who will have had no idea what they were doing for the last few decades, and the plan they were contributing to has proven to be a bust. There will be those who have invested (because they *really* know what they were doing) in trades in Japan's Nikkei stock exchange index and exotica such as this, and have done well.

These professionals will be few and far between, however. What will happen here?

Will *all* private plans be agglomerated with SS and all sorts of other plans so that the plan holders will now be "fully protected" against what might happen when the plan is drawn down to pay for retirement needs? I don't know (fairly obviously), but I would guess that only those who have lost money or who do not have enough assets for their pension will be rescued.

However, it is quite possible that with out-of-control federal spending, the "winners" here might be obliged to purchase US federal bonds as some sort of act of solidarity. If there is the bond crisis occurring at that time (as I have written about in the past), this might be akin to a form of confiscation of financial assets. If the overall situation is as bad as all of this implies, then we may see something along these lines. A desperate Washington will go after the money where they can find it.

To sum all of this up succinctly, let me say that I am sorry. Apart from a few company pension plans and a precious few individuals who really know what they are doing, the vast majority of Americans (and people elsewhere, as what happens in the United States tends to be reflected across the globe) are going to have a series of unpleasant surprises come the age of

65 (probably 70 or higher in reality, although governments seem to be so slow in recognizing the age factor here). A mess, to be sure, and I do not see how the rules of math can be realigned to make it all go away. That ship has unfortunately sailed.

Well, that's it for all of my ponderings on what *is* happening. I just wanted all of my readers to have an idea about everything I have been writing about (and I could have gone on for much longer with so many other problems in the world) and how all of this *will* affect them. It is just a question of when.

Now let's sum it up in a brief epilogue and then let you think—for yourselves please, and not what the press is telling you and has been telling you for your entire life. That ship has also sailed, and it is time for you to *think for yourselves!*

Epilogue
Is All of What Has Been Written in the Book Enough for You?

All kidding aside, I want to thank you for taking your time to have a look at what I have put to paper in the four segments of this book. Simply put, I have had something to say based on my fifty-two years in this business. Well, perhaps that is a touch exaggerated, but it was in winter 1962 when a known user of technical analysis (the study of charts, moving averages, price patterns of various descriptions, Gann Lines, you name it) took me aside and tried to show me what "lines on a bit of paper" could teach me about what markets would be likely to do.

Hamilton Bolton was one of the first in Canada to use these very profitably, and while my father thought I was too young to appreciate what I was being shown, I can still recall the brief lecture he gave me. I shall always be grateful to "Hammy" (as my family called him) for putting the seed into my mind, and today I can use what the price patterns are telling all who wish to listen about the demand for stocks (or anything else) really is.

In other words, technical analysis shows us what the informed money is doing in any given market at any given time. If you wish to know how to invest in stocks for your retirement plan, this is how to do it: look at what the long-term players are doing (the price patterns will always tell you that) and simply ride their coattails! It is simple—*if* you leave your emotions out of it. This last factor, by the way, is why so many traders simply cannot trade when it comes to handling their own money. They cannot be emotionally detached, and so they form part of the seventeen (or nineteen) out of twenty who lose money, often quite a lot of it, when they try something in the market.

I have admittedly written most of this book from an American perspective. No, I am not an American, but I have been living geographically close to that country for most of my life, so I have a good idea of what is important there. It is true that most of the readers of this book will probably be from there, but that merely makes my task a touch easier. Yes, I am writing for everybody in the world, as the problems we face are universal, but the US reader will see all of this much more comprehensively.

Global population growth has been, as I have tried to point out, very uneven, and I am most concerned that the hopelessly overindebted corporations and nations will simply not be able to service their growing debts as the coming years pass. There are simply too many retiring baby boomers and not enough workers to replace them. How, if debts are to be serviced efficiently (and that is very much an open question in my mind), is this to be rectified? It can't, even with all of the tax and accounting gimmicks that stressed governments are going to dream up.

I also wanted to share with you some thoughts I was guided to find from the Bible. I somewhat irreverently called them Fibonacci/pi and wondered if you would like additional slices of this pi as I went forward. The idea behind all of this was to show you that there is indeed something (or someone) behind what makes up our overall historical cycles.

What terrifies me (to be quite honest) is that there are the most incredible things awaiting us in the not too distant future. Marty Armstrong, whom I think very highly of, as you may have noticed, has worked out all of this using economic cycles, and I was absolutely staggered to see that what is in the Bible agrees with his efforts—and possibly even more exactly, to boot! There is clearly something coming, and with these cycles, which I put in the early part of this book, we now have a reasonable idea as to where and when they will hit. If one looks at these pi cycles in conjunction with the book of Revelation ... well, one does indeed have something to think about.

There are many readers who will take exception to all of this, and that is fine and dandy by me. I wrote this book to make people veer away from being told what is happening and how it is all going to play out (again, why seventeen or nineteen out of twenty traders lose money) because I want people to think for themselves. They will need to do so. I think Fibonacci/pi gives them this opportunity.

One of the major things I have been following, and shall continue to do so, is the biggest story for decades, and that is a possible merger between Canada and the United States. The more I think about it, the more likely I think that it is really going to happen. I am not sure of the timing (no,

Fibonacci/pi does not help matters any here), but there will be telltale signs that something is in the works.

The initial something would be a manipulation of the USD/CAD currency exchange rate. If the ongoing merger between once-ancient nation states in Europe continues as it has been (although I do not believe that this will progress as is currently envisioned, as the current crop of leaders there seem to be utterly incompetent as regards getting a plan together and then sticking to it), we may have a template for a North American/NAFTA merger. At the end of the last century (the twentieth, in case you have forgotten) the currencies of the countries slated to join the new euro were maintained by the central banks in a tight trading range. I think this will be the same with the USD/CAD exchange rate. Watch and see!

So overall we can say that there are incredible things going to happen in North America. This makes sense, given that the US dollar is the world's reserve currency, despite some tentative steps away from it by Russia and China. Therefore, I shall watch and observe, and I pray that you will too. It can never hurt and may actually help you a very great deal. I hope so, and if it does, you will indeed be able to answer the title of this book because you will know what *is* happening.

Good luck!

TRUE DIRECTIONS
An affiliate of Tarcher Books

OUR MISSION

Tarcher's mission has always been to publish books
that contain great ideas. Why? Because:

GREAT LIVES BEGIN WITH GREAT IDEAS

At Tarcher, we recognize that many talented authors, speakers,
educators, and thought-leaders share this mission and deserve to be
published—many more than Tarcher can reasonably publish ourselves.
True Directions is ideal for authors and books that increase awareness,
raise consciousness, and inspire others to live their ideals and passions.

Like Tarcher, True Directions books are designed to do three things:
inspire, inform, and motivate.

Thus, True Directions is an ideal way for these important voices
to bring their messages of hope, healing, and help to the world.

Every book published by True Directions—whether it is non-
fiction, memoir, novel, poetry or children's book—continues
Tarcher's mission to publish works that bring positive
change in the world. We invite you to join our mission.

For more information, see the True Directions website:
www.iUniverse.com/TrueDirections/SignUp

Be a part of Tarcher's community to bring positive change
in this world! See exclusive author videos, discover
new and exciting books, learn about upcoming events,
connect with author blogs and websites, and more!
www.tarcherbooks.com

TRUE DIRECTIONS
AN AFFILIATE OF TARCHER BOOKS